# The Twisted Sisters Sock Workbook

## LYNNE VOGEL

INTERWEAVE PRESS

# To Bob and Gladys

Project editor: Rita Buchanan
Technical editor: Jean Lampe
Illustrations: Gayle Ford
Photography: Jim Ann Howard and Lynne Vogel, as noted, Tim Klassen (page 4), Peggy Walsh (back cover)
Cover and page design: Bren Frisch
Production: Dean Howes
Copy editor: Kathryn Banks
Proofreader and indexer: Nancy Arndt

 Interweave Press, Inc.
201 East Fourth Street
Loveland, Colorado 80537-5655
www.interweave.com

Printed in China through Asia Pacific Offset

Library of Congress Cataloging-in-Publication Data

Vogel, Lynne, 1952-
    The twisted sisters sock workbook : dyeing, painting, spinning, designing,
knitting / Lynne Vogel.
            p.  cm.
Includes index.
    ISBN 1-931499-16-0
    1.  Socks. 2.  Knitting—Patterns. 3.  Hand spinning. 4.  Dyes and dyeing—
Textile fibers.  I. Title.
    TT825 .V66 2002
    746.43'20432—dc21

                        2002005721

10  9   8   7   6   5   4

*J*oining **COLORS**, joining hands

interlacing woven strands,

linking **tones** in loops and bands.

Fine techniques from **FOREIGN LANDS**

bring together our *love* of color.

**PAST AND FUTURE** now combined

in a universal language

that will stand the test of time.

this book has been
**Donated**
in
**Loving
Memory**
of

Candace Lyn Johnson

It is truly impossible to bring a work together without the help of many people. The spirit of goodwill has prevailed and each and every person involved deserves the highest blessings of joy that come from such cooperation. To all of you the very finest and most heartfelt thanks.

First and foremost, I'd like to thank my editor, Rita Buchanan, for initiating me into "bookdom" in righteous fashion. I couldn't have done it without her encouragement, knowledge, enthusiasm, teaching, wisdom, patience, humor, and friendship. I can't write THANKS big enough!

Thanks to all at Interweave Press, especially to Marilyn and Amy for getting jazzed about the book in the first place, to Betsy and Bren for the fantastic cover idea, to Gayle for her great illustrations and to Jean Lampe for her microscopically accurate tech editing. You are all so wonderful to work with. To Kathryn Alexander, many thanks for the permission to include your work on energized singles. Your love of your work is contagious.

Big thanks to my photographer, Jim Ann Howard, for the gorgeous shots. Your sense of humor is boundless. Thanks to all whose feet showed in socks: Kami Bruner, Claire Reishman, Ann Griffin, Pam VanDyke, Emily Wright-Tempko; and the cover girls, Julie and Flora Jones, Annie, Meg, Sarah, and Janet Armour-Jones, and Lizzie Clark Duncan (Jones). Big thanks to Boo Rather for lending us her high-powered camera and for her help with the cover shot. Thanks also to Annie Armour and Danielle Stevens for selflessly lending me their digital cameras for lengthy periods of time. And special thanks to Peggy Walsh for capturing my likeness for the back cover.

Thanks to all the technically oriented people who have brought me up to speed in computerland: Walter Castle and Anne Giles for major support and instruction; Andrew Moser and Leigh Burger for a crash course in Photoshop; Dean at Interweave for his patient instruction; Latham Davis for teaching me how to use a slide scanner; and Pradip Malde for letting me sit in on a couple of digital art classes.

Thanks to Mary Kaiser for reading the manuscript with knowledge, wit, and genuine interest. Also thanks to my neighbors, Mary and Dianne, for trying my sock pattern and giving me their feedback. And to my niece, Holly Jean, who invented her own style of casting on within a week of learning how to knit.

Of course, I can't forget my massage therapist, Colette.

Biggest thanks are in order for all the Twisted Sisters for getting jazzed

## THANKS

and staying jazzed and for sending me their hard work for who knows how long. The spirit of the book really lives in all of you! Kudos to Sandy who dyed a living room full of fiber for the Sisters to dive into. May there always be color in your hands.

Thanks also to Rosemary Wilkinson for traveling halfway round the world and donating her wonderful wool and yarn for the dyeing chapter.

I would never have made it without James who graciously and with unfailing humor endured me through the birthing of the book by making me go for woods walks with Monk and Bailey, by cooking more than usual, and by refusing to let me get too serious.

And I'd also like to thank myself for not self-destructing.

# TABLE *of* CONTENTS

# WHO ARE THE
# TWISTED SISTERS?

The Twisted Sisters probably took shape in the mind of "Twisted Mother" Sandy Sitzman well before the group was ever formed. Now the "Millennium Queen Enabler of Prospective and Realized Fiber Addicts," Sandy has been sharing her love of dyeing, spinning, color, and all things fiber for years. She has developed a naturally intuitive, non-threatening teaching style that encourages minimum sweat and maximum enjoyment.

Those of us who respond better to simple, learn-by-doing methods delight in this method of teaching. We respond by leaps and bounds where before we had stubbornly resisted. Our interest grows and we branch out into other skills, learning them with ease and excitement. Eventually some of us even move on to more scientific and technique-oriented methods once we wish to refine or reproduce our results. But even from the earliest stages, we learn skills that delight us for the sheer enjoyment of doing them.

photo: Jim Ann Howard

▶ Front row, left to right: Alina Egerman, Lynne Vogel, Rachael Hocking, Jan Prewitt. Back row, left to right: Sandy Sitzman, Laurie Weinsoft, Linda Berning, Jane Penny, Lynn Nagasako, Gail Marracci, Stephanie Prewitt.

Sandy's ability to teach this way opened the door to many women who wished to enhance their knitting experience with the color, texture, and life of handspun yarns. Her generous nature and noncompetitive spirit taught us cooperation. Her calm, methodical approach helped to tame creative dragons and provided a focused setting for expressing wild dreams of color.

Soon a group took shape, meeting each year at the Black Sheep Gathering in Eugene, Oregon, where Sandy had sold her hand-dyed fibers since 1990. Once a day trip for some, it became a weekend-long event. Sandy booked a group of rooms and we would come with our wheels and spin late into the night. Ministering angel, Jeanne Roll, would make sure everyone received an annual foot rub while we caught up with friends we sometimes only saw once a year. Events expanded to a bi-yearly beach retreat and a holiday party. Our connections deepened and our friendships grew. We learned more skills and enjoyed the ones we knew by heart. Now we are the Twisted Sisters.

We Sisters are busy women and several of us have very demanding jobs, but we still find time to do what we want. It may take a while, but we accomplish wonderful things, and you can, too.

I want to thank all the Sisters for their undying enthusiasm and support. Thanks for going out of your way to dye, spin, and knit the wonderful socks in this book. It wouldn't be the Twisted Sisters sock book without you. Special thanks to Sandy for being beside me every step of the way.

**The Twisted Sisters include:**

Linda Berning: Owner, NW Wools, Portland, Oregon

Alina Egerman: Hospice nurse

Cindy Granlund: Full-time nursing student

Rachael Hocking: Organic farmer

Gail Marracci: Postdoctoral fellow working in multiple sclerosis research

Lynn Nagasako: Assistant Attorney General, Oregon Department of Justice, specializing in finance

Gina Parosa: Antique knitting machine expert, full-time mother of three

Jane Penny: Hospice nurse

Jan Prewitt: Attorney, Oregon Department of Justice

Stephanie Prewitt: High school chemistry teacher

Debby Schnabel: Fiber artist and neonatal nurse

Sandy Sitzman: Spinning and dyeing instructor, owner of Woolgatherings, home of the Happy Socks Kit

Lynne Vogel: Fiber artist, author, and therapeutic bodyworker

Laurie Weinsoft: Finance and operations manager, Boydstun Metal Works, Inc; spinning instructor and shopkeeper at NW Wools

And ministering angel, Jeanne Roll: Therapeutic touch practitioner and retired nurse

# COLOR *and* DYEING

**COLOR IS ONE** of the most powerful means of nonverbal expression. Single colors move us in such a primal way we may not be able to explain our feelings about them. Combinations of colors express sheer exuberance, comfort, fiery energy, confusion, clarity, all sorts of feelings with a directness that can't be achieved in words. You may not even know quite what it is you want to say, but somehow, with color one can express the inexpressible.

Although we may choose a single color as a favorite, it rarely stands alone and by the nature of reality must exist beside other colors. This is why hand-painted, multicolored rovings seem so appealing. Whether they are a balanced

photo: Tim Klassen

Sandy chooses the colors she loves from her well-tended garden and knits several colorways at once using Fair Isle techniques. The Merino/Tencel® fiber shimmers like raindrops.

photo: Jim Ann Howard

Jane spun very long sections of solid colors from Sandy's Fruit Salad roving and then Navajo-plied the singles to duplicate the primal blaze of the original roving with these beautiful broad bands of pure color. She won the 2000 Reserve Grand Champion award in the Fiber Arts Division at the Black Sheep Gathering for this yarn.

blend of harmonious shades or a wild splash of primary colors, they grab the eye immediately. The challenge is to use them in a way that brings out their best qualities, retains their freshness, and captures the essence that attracted us to them in the first place.

Before I ever learned to spin I was fascinated by multicolored yarns. I spent many years finding ways to use them to their best advantage. I loved the way they lent depth and movement to a piece, softened edges, or picked up colors from different sections and tied them together harmoniously. But I never just sat down and knitted a whole ball into a sweater because it would come out striped, usually in little random stripes that looked like mistakes rather than serendipity. Once I took up sock knitting, I began using those yarns more and more. Because of the sock's small size, the colors staged out in a pleasing and ever fascinating way.

The photos throughout this book show how I and other knitters work with multicolored rovings and yarns. As you flip through, note the effects you really love. Make socks for yourself; make them as a special gift for someone else.

Maybe you've wanted to do

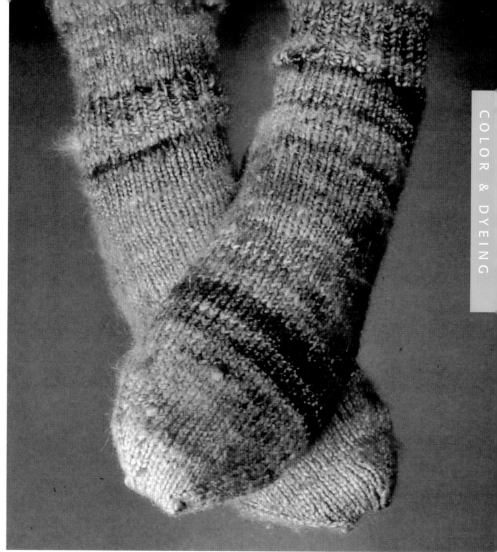

photo: Jim Ann Howard

▲ Lynne blends colors very slowly from one shade to the next by knitting with an assortment of yarns that share similar color elements.

something different or something special and for one reason or another, you've put it off. Now is the time to pull out all those magical inspirations, dust them off, and bring them to life. Don't compromise on your enthusiasm, and don't worry if the socks will be really wearable or if they will match anything. They should be expressions of your inspiration alone. This doesn't necessarily mean that they have to be wild. They can be as subtle and mysterious as you wish. If you work from your inspiration, you can't help but love the outcome.

Dyeing fiber and yarn with pour-dye methods is a quick way to get a handpainted look. Although it is possible to get good results as a beginner in these techniques, there is a lot of room for refinement, and a high level of control and expertise can be achieved with practice and experience. Also, dyeing can be fun. I didn't realize this until Twisted Mother Sandy invited me into her kitchen to learn her pour-dye methods. In my mind I felt like I was being dragged kicking and screaming to perform some horrible tedious task, but I emerged calm and confident. Why? She taught me to dye in an intuitive manner. Her method was spontaneous, designed for immediate gratification with little sweat and lots of color. No measuring, no anxiety, just pour and see what happens. Once I learned the basics this way, I began to hone my own technique using scientific methods when I chose, but I have always come back to working intuitively, especially when developing an inspiration.

The only real differences between scientific and intuitive methods of working are precise measurement and documentation. If I wanted to dye some fiber by scientific method, I would first weigh my fiber accurately and write down the weight. Then I'd soak the fiber for a prescribed amount of time in a certain temperature of water. All my dyes would be mixed according to the accurate weight of dye per volume of water. I would painstakingly measure all dye before I applied it, writing down everything as I went along. Then I would control my dyebath or steam bath with a thermometer and a timer. I would let the fiber cool for an exact period of time, and then I'd wash it in a precise temperature of water and hang it to dry under controlled conditions. What would I hope to gain from all this? Reproducible results. This would come in very handy if I wanted to work in large volumes and make many successive, consistent dyelots and have perfect fastness to each color. There isn't anything wrong with this, but it takes time and effort that isn't necessary when learning to have fun dyeing a few rovings for socks.

It is possible to get absolutely beautiful results in small quantities simply by being fairly consistent. When mixing dye solutions, I always use the same size jars and the same amount of dye powder. I learned fairly quickly how wet my fiber should feel and how much to dilute my dyes to get light colors. I discovered how to judge the temperature of the dyebath by the amount of steam rising above the surface. I could tell when it was about to boil just by listening. I could see the dyebath becoming clear and learned when to add more dye if needed. Before long, I even learned how much stock solution to pour in to make a certain depth of shade. This freed me to work spontaneously. I could have fun and just pour! A little of this and a bit of that and voila! A beautiful roving.

Photo: Jim Ann Howard

◀ Rachel spun these two beautiful Blue-faced Leicester rovings for the sock shown on p. 56. Sandy dyed the roving above, Lynne the one below.
*Amelia handspindle from Hatchtown Farm.*

As I began to dye by the intuitive method, my results were largely irreproducible. I invariably had to come back and make a little more of a slightly different shade or color. But I discovered wonderful things purely by accident and never got the same effect twice. What's the advantage? I began to use many more colors than I originally intended. Running out of yarn became an opportunity rather than a disaster. The more colors I used, the richer my knitting became. My work began to have a life of its own that mimicked nature in its infinite variations. Like the intriguing meanderings in naturally dyed Persian rugs, each color became precious because it was unique and I truly treasured my work.

I emphasize socks in this book because small projects are a perfect focus for designers of all levels. They take less

I *really* made the most progress when I decided not to FEAR FAILURE. This freed me to pour with abandon and my results were BOLDER *and* more exciting to me than ever before.

— SANDY'S TIP

Lynne dyed two totally different colorways, then plied them for this irresistible ball of yarn.

Photo: Jim Ann Howard

time and materials. Because socks can be completed so quickly, you can work with unusual or seldom-used color combinations and not waste months on something you've been eager to try. When the socks are done, it's on to another wonderful color combo. After you work out all the elements in miniature, you can carefully plan a larger project along similar lines with much more confidence.

## A PERSONAL APPROACH TO COLOR

I love to work with handpainted rovings and yarns because they are so quick and fun to dye and so endlessly enjoyable to spin and knit. After I choose and mix my colors, I pour them onto a length of fiber or yarn and steam. Once the fiber is dry I can make simple socks and let the yarn do all the work.

I find the most enjoyable part, the most deeply satisfying part of the process, is choosing and mixing the colors. I usually work in a thematic way, using the colors I find on a woods walk or a day at the beach. I'll have a name for the experience in mind before I even begin mixing, like Zinnias, Tide Pools, or Autumn Leaves. Mixing these color combinations and eventually wearing them brings me into close harmony with

nature's beauty. I actually imagine wearing them to the place that originally inspired me.

Since color theory can be frightening to many people and analysis of hue value and saturation can send the strongest running for cover, my intention is to encourage those without a fine arts background by using plain language in place of scientific terminology. Perhaps this will open new doors to the fascinating yet enigmatic world of color.

Color appreciation begins with observation. It is a very personal tool because no two people have exactly the same way of seeing or naming color. An entire science designed to measure the "temperature" of light has evolved from this phenomenon. All I want to do is have some fun dyeing, spinning, and knitting, so those measurements simply don't concern me. What interests me is beauty.

Any color can be analyzed in terms of three qualities. To learn more about these basic qualities of color without verbal intrusion, you can practice manipulating them on your home computer, either in the control panel or in any simple graphic program.

Variation of lightness (value): Every color has a value of light or shadow. Different shades of blue jeans are a perfect example of this. Some are deep indigo, some medium, and some very pale, but they are all indigo. Black and white represent the most possible contrast between dark and light.

Variation of color (hue): Very simply, the colors of the rainbow. Each color is a unique wavelength of light.

Variation of brightness (saturation): Lime green and sage green differ in brightness. They are both green, but one is brilliant, one somber. ☼

As I look out the window on this summer day in Tennessee, I see a sea of green. There are yellow, olive, pine, and forest greens in the hemlocks, that indescribable dark tannin green in the oaks, deep bluish greens in the ivy and wisteria vines, and mellow moss green on the trunks of the trees. These many greens all blend into a harmonious whole. Yet not one of these colors comes in a dye powder straight off the shelf. If I want to surround my feet with the verdant summer forest, I have a little mixing to do.

### PREPARING DYE STOCK SOLUTIONS

The dyes I use, called Sabraset® or Lanaset® dyes, are available from craft suppliers (see p. 90). I buy a basic set of eight colors (yellow, gold, turquoise, blue, red, scarlet, violet, and black), then create an unlimited palette by mixing.

These dyes are sold as very concentrated powders that keep for years if stored dry at room temperature. Before use, they must be dissolved in water to make what's called a stock solution. Once dye powders are dissolved in water, they can be freely intermixed and are easy and fun to use. All Sabraset® and Lanaset® colors are completely intermixable with each other and give a wide range of both brilliant colors and muted, natural looking colors.

Other dyes are available, but I prefer these because they are easy to blend when pouring directly on fiber, I like the color range, and they are fast (that is, they don't fade due to light or bleed in the wash). So all the formulas I give are specifically for Sabraset® and Lanaset® dyes.

Scientific-type dyers prepare a 1 percent stock solution by mixing 1 gram of dye with 100 ml of water, but if you don't have a scale or a metric measuring cup you can just follow this simple formula instead:

**Mix 2 level teaspoons of dye powder into 1 quart (0.95 liters) of very hot or boiling water.**

It is more important to make the same strength of solution every time than to have the strength be exactly 1 percent. I mix all colors the same strength except yellow and scarlet. For yellow, I use 4 teaspoons of dye powder (twice the standard amount). For scarlet, I use 3 teaspoons of dye powder per 1 quart (0.95 l) of water.

In a quart (0.95 l) mason jar or plastic container, thoroughly wet, or "paste," the dye powder with a tablespoon of very hot or boiling water. I usually paste the dye in a plastic measuring cup with a broad bottom and prefer a plastic mayonnaise spreader or spatula for pasting because it has a flexible flat surface that really mashes the powder. Also, even though it takes on color, the plastic washes clean and the color doesn't come off into subsequent mixings. Wooden tools absorb dye and will contaminate other colors, especially yellow, so if you prefer wooden tools use a different one for each color.

After preparing the paste, slowly add the rest of the very hot or boiling water, stirring continually in order to fully dissolve the powder.

Label each jar with the color name and date. If you live in an earthquake-prone area, think about storing your dyes in plastic. Store stock solutions in a cool dark place out of the reach of children. Most solutions will keep for at least six months.

Always stir a stock solution before using it to make sure all the dye particles are in suspension. No matter how well you dissolve the dye when you prepare the solution, some will always settle out when it is at rest.

**MIXING COLORS** Mixing colors is full of fun and discovery. Very often we find beautiful shades by happy accident. Experimentation is the key to success because results depend on so many factors: the strength and proportion of the solutions, the heat and acidity applied, and the particular batch of fiber or yarn.

I like to mix dyes in transparent containers so I can gently swirl the liquid and see the result like stained glass against the side of the container. I often dot a drop of dye onto a white paper towel to check for color and intensity. This gives me a relative idea of the final outcome,

▶ Lynne tested the Tide Pool dye colors on this paper towel.

but since these dyes are made for wool and animal fibers, they never look truly accurate on plant fiber.

Some guesswork is an inescapable part of the process. Like playing a musical instrument, only practice will give you a true handle on the medium. In the meantime, beautiful results happen often, even if they don't exactly match your original intention. With experience, you can come very close to your vision.

Pour-dye techniques are methods of directly applying color to fiber. Therefore, it is important to mix the desired colors in the proper strengths before applying the dyes. The stock solutions give intense colors, so mixing is required to make pastels, somber shades, deep tones, or wispy light colors. All mixing is done with dyes in solution. Here are some guidelines and tips.

**Dye strength** Different dye colors have different mixing power (see box, p. 10). Take this into consideration when figuring proportions. For instance, to mix a

photo: Jim Ann Howard

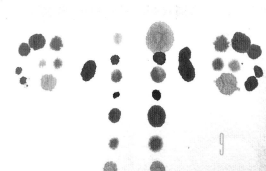

## MIXING PALE, PASTEL, AND DARK SHADES

| Dye color (mixed in stock solution) (L) = Lanaset name (S) = Sabraset name | Pale shade (made by mixing 1 part dye stock with 2 parts water) | Pastel shade (made by mixing 1 part dye stock with 1 part water) | Dark shade (made by mixing 4 parts dye stock with 1 part black stock) |
|---|---|---|---|
| Bordeaux (L) | lavender pink | mauve pink | deep plum |
| Red (L) | carnation pink | medium pink | deep blood red |
| Scarlet (L) | peachy pink | watermelon pink | dark mandarin red |
| Orange (L) | pale peach | peach | rust |
| Gold (L) | yellowish tan | sandy apricot | olive green |
| Sun yellow (S) | maize | buttercup | chartreuse |
| Teal green (L) | mint green | jade green | forest spruce |
| Turquoise (L) | light turquoise | medium turquoise | Prussian blue |
| Blue (L) | sky blue | medium cobalt | navy blue |
| Navy (L) | light blue gray | soft periwinkle | midnight blue |
| Violet (L) | lavender | orchid violet | deep royal purple |
| Brown (L) | tan | medium burnt umber | tarnished bronze |

kelly green, you use approximately one part turquoise and two parts yellow, because turquoise is stronger than yellow. If you're in doubt about a color's strength, start mixing by slowly adding the darker color into the lighter one. Add just a few drops at a time.

**Light colors** Pale or light colors are the easiest to achieve. Mix one part stock solution to one part water to make a medium pastel shade; mix one part stock solution to two or three parts water to make a pale shade. Of course there are infinite variations in between, but all colors become lighter with the addition of water. The lighter the color, the more liberally you can pour.

**Dark colors** These colors can be made several ways, each yielding different results. Mix a color with black and the color will become dark and dull with a decided grayness. These colors are reminiscent of nighttime or storms. Gold or mustard plus black makes a wonderful olive drab.

Make a double-strength stock solution of darker colors like red and violet and the resulting dark shade, poured undiluted, will be vibrant and deep, such as a deep blood red or a deep royal

purple. Use these dark colors carefully, for they are very strong and can easily bleed to lighter areas.

Mix a medium color, such as green, with a darker color, such as violet, and the green will become somber yet natural, like the shadowed tones found in dense shrubbery.

**Muted, natural colors** Muted colors that remind us of our natural surroundings are achieved by intermixing colors that lie some distance from each other on the color wheel. A color that is mixed in equal parts with the color directly opposite on the color wheel should, in theory, make gray or black. This rarely happens. Most of the time the product of these combinations is more brown than gray, but the principle is still very useful.

An aqua color much like the stone, Persian turquoise, can be made by adding a small amount of orange to turquoise dye and adding some water for a pastel shade. The orange softens the brilliance of the turquoise dye and makes it very natural looking.

To take the edge off bright pink (diluted red), add a few drops of diluted lime green (made with four parts yellow to one part turquoise with water

## MIXING STRENGTH OF THE BASIC DYE COLORS

| Lanaset® Dyes | Sabraset® Dyes |
|---|---|
| Black | Black |
| Navy | Navy |
| Brown | Rust brown |
| Violet | Violet |
| Turquoise | Turquoise |
| Blue | Royal blue |
| Teal | Emerald |
| Bordeaux | Magenta |
| Red | Deep red |
| Scarlet | Scarlet |
| Orange | Not available |
| Gold | Mustard |
| Yellow | Sun yellow |

⚠ Some dye colors are more powerful than others. Keep this in mind when choosing proportions to mix together. These lists arrange the dye colors in order from strong (at the top) to weak (at the bottom) and give the Lanaset® and Sabraset® names for equivalent colors.

added). Scarlet and turquoise in equal proportions make a groovy grape shade, while scarlet and teal in similar proportions make eggplant. If you are trying to mix a particular shade and it looks like it needs a certain color, add it drop by drop until you get what you want.

**DYEING A COLOR WHEEL** To make this color wheel, we dyed roving in twelve colors. These spectral colors, or the pure colors of the rainbow that are found on the outer ring of this color wheel, were made with the formulas given below. To mix brilliant, clear colors, we chose colors closest to each other on the color wheel. For instance, turquoise and yellow make a brighter green than blue and yellow.

The muted shades on the inner ring of this wheel were made by carding. Each pure color was combined with a small amount of its complement, the color that lies directly opposite to it on the wheel. Muted shades can also be achieved by mixing dye solutions in similar proportions.

Following are the formulas for the twelve spectral colors. We used Lanaset® dyes, mixed in standard stock solutions (see p. 8) of 2 teaspoons dye powder per 1 quart (0.95 l) of hot water, except for yellow (use 4 teaspoons of dye) and scarlet (use 3 teaspoons of dye).

▶ Lynne and Sandy used Lanaset® dyes on Blue-faced Leicester roving to create this color wheel.

**Yellow:** Pure yellow stock solution.

**Yellow-orange:** One part orange to one part yellow.

**Orange:** Pure orange stock solution.

**Red-orange:** One part orange to one part scarlet.

**Red:** Pure scarlet stock solution.

**Red-violet:** One part scarlet, one part violet, one part water.

**Violet:** Pure violet stock solution.

**Blue-violet:** One part violet, one part blue.

**Blue:** Pure blue stock solution.

**Blue-green:** One part turquoise, one part teal.

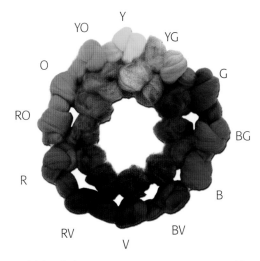

photo: Lynne Vogel

photo: Lynne Vogel

▲ Debby spun Blue-faced Leicester roving dyed with the color wheel hues for this striking cuff, choosing motifs from Alice Starmore's *Charts for Colour Knitting*. She felt that using all the colors in equal measures would be too intense, so she reserved yellow, yellow-orange, and orange for accent. She spun two color sequences—red, red-violet, purple, and blue-violet, and blue, blue-green, green, and yellow-green— then Navajo-plied them to keep the colors solid. She worked a Fair Isle pattern with the two yarns.

**Green:** One part turquoise, two parts yellow.

**Yellow-green:** One part green (above), two parts yellow.

**DEVELOPING A THEMATIC COLOR SCHEME** Color schemes found in nature are naturally harmonious. I enjoy mixing a symbiotic color combination by choosing a theme from nature and selecting a group of colors I have observed relating to that theme. Since I have spent a lot of time snooping around in tide pools, I have chosen this as my example. The colors of tide pools greatly depend on the time of day and weather conditions, and I can capture different effects by choosing different dyeing techniques as I go along.

I start by mixing a general group of colors that remind me of tide pools. I

## DYE FORMULAS FOR MIXING THE TIDE POOL COLORS

To create the Tide Pool colors, I started with standard stock solutions (see p. 8) and combinations prepared as for the color wheel (see p. 11), then mixed them in the following proportions.

**Blue-green:** 1 cup (240 ml) turquoise stock, 1 cup (240 ml) teal stock.

**Aqua:** 1 cup (240 ml) blue-green stock, 3 tablespoons (45 ml) orange stock.

**Turquoise:** standard stock.

**Diluted turquoise:** 1 cup (240 ml) turquoise stock, 1 cup water (240 ml).

**Shaded orchid:** 1 cup (240 ml) red-violet, 2 tablespoons (30 ml) violet stock, ¼ (60 ml) cup yellow-green, ½ cup (120 ml) water.

**Coral:** 2 cups (480 ml) red-orange, 2 tablespoons (30 ml) turquoise, ½ cup (120 ml) water.

**Diluted coral:** 1 cup (240 ml) coral (above), 1 cup water (240 ml).

**Muted coral:** 1 cup (240 ml) coral (above), 1 tablespoon (15 ml) turquoise stock.

**Diluted muted coral:** 1 cup (240 ml) muted coral (above), 1 cup water (240 ml).

**Kelp:** ½ cup (120 ml) gold stock, 3 tablespoons (45 ml) red-violet stock, 3 tablespoons (45 ml) yellow-green.

**Sun rays:** ½ cup (120 ml) gold stock, ½ cup (120 ml) yellow stock, 1 tablespoon (15 ml) muted coral (above), a few drops shaded orchid (above).

Photo: Jim Ann Howard

All the rovings and yarns shown in these photos are dyed with Tide Pool colors. The different dye methods produce different results.

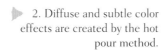 1. Brilliant colors can be achieved with the cold pour method.

have included formulas for the colors used in this combination as an illustration of color mixing (see box, p. 12). I don't go by formulas myself, but just mix by approximate proportion as I go along. For instance, if I think a coral color I have mixed is too bright, I mute it with a bit of an opposite or nearly opposite color on the color wheel, such as turquoise or teal. Many colors in nature are muted to some degree, and it helps to have an idea about how to mix them.

It's important to combine colors in different amounts. If I used equal proportions of all the colors I mixed, the resulting yarn would not look like tide pools, but like something else. To describe my theme in a realistic manner, I choose a predominant color and use the others as accents. Choosing a predominant color also helps to make a roving that stays fresh looking when spun.

Photo: Jim Ann Howard

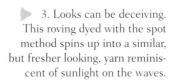 2. Diffuse and subtle color effects are created by the hot pour method.

Photo: Jim Ann Howard

3. Looks can be deceiving. This roving dyed with the spot method spins up into a similar, but fresher looking, yarn reminiscent of sunlight on the waves.

photo: Lynne Vogel

These skeins of Falklands wool yarn from Rosemary Wilkinson were dyed with different methods. Top: Aqua dye was poured on this skein in a cold dyebath and then brought up to 190°F (88°C) before adding other colors. It is somber and murky, like the shadows of the tide pools. Middle: This skein was brought up to 190°F (88°C) before dye was applied. The pH of the dyebath was about 3.7, a bit too acid, and the dye hit very rapidly without bleeding to surrounding colors. A few light places show, but the yarn looks fresh and pretty. Bottom: Yarn dyed with the cold pour method is similar, but the colors are deeper and more even.

Depending on what color I emphasize, I can focus on different elements of the theme. For instance, to focus on the actual pools, I would use blue tones as the predominant color and dye at least half of my fiber, maybe a bit more, in turquoise and aqua. I would intersperse the other colors as accents to balance the theme. To focus on corals, I would make the coral colors predominant and accent with the other colors. To focus on kelp, I would mix a few more muted greens and browns and make them predominant, and since both kelp and sea grass have a long, slender shape, I would intersperse the other colors more often than for pools or coral.

## GENERAL GUIDELINES ON DYEING

The dye methods presented in this book

photos: Lynne Vogel

are called *pour-dyeing* because they involve pouring dye solutions directly onto wet fiber. The hot pour method requires heating the fiber in a vessel before pouring on the dye. Cold pour techniques involve pouring dye onto unheated fiber which is laid out on plastic wrap, then wrapping and steaming the "painted" fiber or yarn to set the dye. All these techniques produce multi-colored fibers and yarns. If you want an even, solid colored yarn, it is best to use an immersion dye method, as described in many other books.

All dyeing instructions in this chapter are specifically for wool, wool blends, and superwash wool, but other protein fibers can be dyed with the same techniques. Superwash is very different from regular wool and takes some special handling, as noted in the directions.

Different fibers—even different breeds of wool—react differently to dyes, so if you dye them together the resulting colors will coordinate but won't match exactly. Likewise, if you dye fiber and yarn at the same time, the colors probably

◀ Lynn Nagasako loves to dye with natural dyes. She tried using the pour methods with natural dye extracts and came up with these beautiful results.

won't match exactly once the fiber is spun into yarn.

I normally use commercially prepared rovings (also called tops) in natural shades of white. If you want to dye wool fleece, homemade preparations, or natural colored wools, try experimenting with these instructions to develop your own techniques.

Yarns of wool and wool blends can also be dyed beautifully. Follow the procedures given for fiber, substituting yarn instead. Since yarn can handle a lot more abuse in the dyeing process without felting than undyed fiber, it makes beginning dyeing fun and easy.

**Mix plenty of dye** I prepare stock solutions in 1-quart (0.95 l) amounts. When mixing dyes, I make at least 1 cup (240 ml) of each color. This is important because it takes at least a few cups of dye to do a batch of roving or yarn. I don't want to run out, as it's hard to remix exactly the same color. Any leftover dye can be saved for future use.

**Weigh out enough fiber** To estimate quantities, weigh the fiber or yarn while it is still dry. It takes a minimum of 4 ounces (113 g) of two-ply sportweight superwash to make a small pair of women's socks in stockinette stitch. Always dye more than you think you will need, and think what wonderful fun things you can do with the leftovers (if you have any). So you should dye 6 ounces (170 g) of wool at the very minimum for small socks and at least 8 ounces (227 g) or more for larger or thicker socks. Fair Isle and mosaic knitting techniques take nearly twice as much yardage as the same yarn knit in plain stockinette.

**Pull off lengths of roving** Wool roving or top comes in a long strand that's usually folded, coiled, or rolled into a ball when you buy it. Look for an end and start there. Measure a piece of roving

There are no ugly *colors*
Many colors that seem ugly to us alone are *indispensable* in COMBINATION. Often they make our FAVORITES seem even *more beautiful.*

— LYNNE'S TIP

about 1 yard (0.91 m) long, grab it firmly with both hands spaced at least a foot (30 cm) apart, and pull your hands apart to separate the roving.

Dyeing takes practice, and that is why I'm suggesting that you use 1-yard (0.91 m) lengths of roving when you try these techniques for the first time. Try successive attempts at the same color combination until you get the hang of how much dye it takes to get the effect you want. Many times, even the bloopers will go with something and what you didn't like can turn out to be something you can use beautifully. An ugly roving can make a beautiful yarn!

**Make yarn into skeins** Yarn must be in a skein for dyeing. If the yarn is already in a skein, make sure that the ends are tied loosely around the skein. Tightly tied ends will resist the dye and leave an undyed spot on the yarn. Retie them if necessary.

If your yarn is in a ball, wind it into a skein. Bring the two yarn ends together and tie them loosely around the skein. (You should be able to insert two fingers under the tie.) Then take a piece of thick, contrasting yarn, double it, and tie it loosely around the other end of the skein. Use this tie to pick up the wet skein in order to avoid tangling the yarn.

**A quick word about felt** Felting is a spinner's worst nightmare. The three factors needed to felt wool are: Alkalinity, Heat, and Agitation. In short, AHA! Any two of these together will lead to trouble, so avoid them in combination. Alkalinity comes from soap. Heat, including any rapid change in temperature for that matter, comes from the sink tap and the dyepot. Agitation comes from the dyer or from the forceful action of water coming out of the sink tap directly onto the fiber. Whenever you are handling wet unspun fiber, be as gentle as possible.

**Wetting, or presoaking** Fiber or yarn must be thoroughly wet before you dye it. The success of your finished product begins with the wetting process. Fill a large vessel such as a dyepot or a bowl with cool water. Use plenty of water

because the fiber will drink up quite a lot. Avoid pouring water directly from the tap onto the fiber because this can cause felting. Here are tips on wetting different fibers:

- Regular wool and wool-blend rovings. Gently press the fiber into the water, pressing out air bubbles as you go. When the fiber has totally submerged and swelled to about twice its former size, it is ready to use. Plain, clean wool becomes wet very quickly.

- Superwash wool roving. Coil the roving loosely as you would a skein of yarn before immersion. This keeps the slippery fibers from floating apart. Resist the urge to squeeze this fiber, but just gently press it down into the water until it begins to soak it up. Let it rest in the water until it is thoroughly wet. When the whiteness of the wool completely fades to a soft fuzzy, pale grayness, as though the fiber was becoming invisible, it is ready to dye.

Coiled superwash roving soaking prior to dyeing.

- Yarn. It takes longer to thoroughly wet yarn than fiber. Wool yarn should soak for at least an hour and can soak all day or overnight without harm.

- Silk. Silk wets more slowly than wool, so if your fiber or yarn contains any silk, wait several hours to be sure it is thoroughly soaked. For hard-to-wet silk, bring silk to a very slow simmer in a dyepot full of water with a few drops of soap or other wetting agent added. This expands the fibers and makes the wetting agent more effective. Cool and rinse before dyeing.

**Washing fiber and yarn after dyeing** After you have dyed the goods, you must wash and rinse them to remove residual dye and acid from the fiber. This is an exciting moment, especially when working with the cold pour method, because it is the unveiling of the final colors. But remember: impatience equals felt. Let the dyed goods cool to room temperature before you proceed. It's like letting your car come to a full stop before you get out.

Photo: Jim Ann Howard

photo: Jim Ann Howard

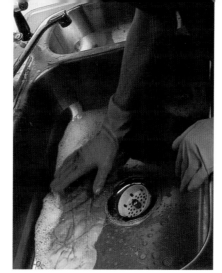

photo: Jim Ann Howard

photo: Jim Ann Howard

⚠ Remove the sink stopper so the liquid can drain freely, and carefully position the fiber between the drain and the corner of the sink where water can flow freely from the tap without actually running onto the fiber itself. Form a dam with the fiber so that the water from the tap builds up behind the fiber mass and causes water to slowly run through the fiber mass, forcing the residual dye towards the drain. If your sink is small, let the water run down the side of the sink wall, so that it doesn't run directly onto the fiber. Press the fiber against the bottom of the sink to speed removal of dye.

⚠ Add a few drops of dishwashing soap to the high water behind the dam and let the flowing water wash the soapy liquid through the fiber mass. Keep pressing the fiber as the soapy water flows through. This will cause the water from behind the dam to flow over the fiber, removing sudsy buildup. Avoid using too much soap because it encourages felting.

⚠ To rinse, repeat this process until the water flowing through the fiber runs clear with no soapy residue. Then lift the roving or yarn from the rinse water and let the water drain out as much as possible while gently squeezing.

To wash roving, use the following steps as a guide. Always handle wet roving by supporting the entire mass. Don't just pick up one end, because the weight of the water can pull the fibers apart. When washing yarn, keep track of the ties that secure the skein. Grab the skein near the tie to prevent tangles.

**Drying** After rinsing, gently place the wet fiber or yarn in the tub of your washing machine, turn off the hoses that feed water to your machine, and set the washer to spin cycle. The centrifugal force of the spin will remove more water from the fiber than any other method. If you don't have a washer, roll the fiber in an old bath towel and press out as much water as possible.

▶ For mixing and storing dyes, you can use recycled plastic containers or order special ones from dye supply houses.

Hang the roving or yarn to dry in an airy spot away from direct sun. Sometimes tiny amounts of residual dye

photo: Jim Ann Howard

17

photo: Jim Ann Howard

Stainless steel bowls and shallow wash pans both work well for the hot pour method. The liquid level should allow the fiber to be covered and just barely float away from the bottom surface. Put just enough fiber in the pan so all of it floats at the surface. Any buried fiber or yarn will not receive the full intensity of the dye. If you want the areas of color to be very distinct, pour small amounts at a time and don't touch the fiber at all. Wiggle the fiber if you want to soften the edges of the colored areas.

remain in the fiber at this point and can drip, so hang the fiber where this won't be a problem or put down old towels or newspaper to catch the drips.

**HOT POUR DYEING** Hot pour dyeing is my favorite method. It's a way to achieve a very soft watercolor effect without a lot of guesswork. In a shallow pan or large stainless steel bowl with a flat bottom, you bring the wetted undyed fiber up to about 190°F (88°C), the temperature at which the dye will strike, then pour the dye onto the fiber. In this way you can pour or "paint" directly onto the wet fiber and have the color stay basically where you put it. Success depends on three factors—temperature, pH, and water level—as noted in the following

directions. These directions refer to roving, but you can use the same technique to dye yarn.

## Procedure

1. Measure or weigh out the amount of fiber or yarn you wish to dye. Presoak it (see p. 16).

2. Prepare some vinegar water by adding about 2 teaspoons (10 ml) of vinegar per gallon (3.8 l) of water. Test the pH and adjust if needed; it should be about pH 4. That means the solution is acidic enough for the dye to strike rapidly. If the solution is too acidic, the dye will strike the surface quickly but not penetrate fully into the roving. The vinegar water solution can be stored indefinitely.

3. Put presoaked fiber into a pan. Add vinegar water to a depth of at least 1½" (3.8 cm). Although you could use this technique with less liquid, it would be very difficult to control the temperature. Using enough liquid is important for good results.

When adding more colors, pour dye solutions next to each other and gently tap the edges to soften the transition.

photo: Jim Ann Howard

## JUDGING WATER TEMPERATURE

Temperature is important in this dyeing technique. If the fiber is not hot enough, the dye will disperse and color the whole roving rather than the part you want dyed. But pay close attention and don't allow the water to boil, as that might felt your roving. Boiling water can also felt wool yarn, but not as quickly. Be especially careful about temperature if you are using a shallow pan with a broad flat bottom, as it will come to a boil very quickly.

Of course you can monitor water temperature with a thermometer. I've learned to judge it by sound. Listen closely, and you'll hear that as water approaches the boiling point, it makes more and more of a groaning noise. Just as it reaches boiling temperature, it makes less of a groaning noise and changes to a hissing noise. Ideally you begin adding dye when the groaning is at its peak.

photo: Jim Ann Howard

4. Slowly bring the dyebath to about 190°F (88°C). There will be steam, but no bubbles rising.

5. From stock solutions, mix the colors you want to use (see p. 9–10) and have them ready in containers that pour easily. When the dyebath is gently simmering, start slowly pouring dye directly onto the fiber. Begin with lighter or brighter colors, adding the deeper or more muted ones after the brighter ones have been absorbed.

6. After adding a color, wait for the fiber to absorb the dye and the water to turn clear. This is called *exhausting* the dye. Then pour another color.

To check the colors, gently pull a small area of the wool out of the water once the dye has fully exhausted and let some of the liquid run out. The wool will dry to an even lighter shade, so take that into consideration as you add dye.

7. Once the fiber has absorbed all the color you want, let it simmer gently, not boiling, for another 10 minutes.

8. Turn off the heat and cool to room temperature.

9. Wash and rinse the fiber and let it dry.

**Tips on controlling colors** Experience is the best teacher, so make mental notes as you dye. Watch what happens as you add colors and note how colors change from the dyepot to the finished fiber or yarn.

☼ The more slowly you work, the more control you have.

☼ Remember that colors mix as they overlap. If you want a more diffuse edge to the color, tap the fiber gently to encourage the dyes to spread out a little.

☼ Tapping also helps if you think it

photo: Jim Ann Howard

This shows the finished roving and yarn spun from it. The subtle color effects are typical of the hot pour method.

### SUPPLIES FOR HOT POUR DYEING

Shallow pan or large stainless steel bowl

Distilled white vinegar

pH paper, acid range

Stirring stick

Dye solutions in easy pouring containers

Syringe (optional)

Wet fiber or yarn

will get too dark where you have poured. The more you tap, the more the color will lighten as it spreads out. It is important to make the colors darker than you want them to turn out, because they will lighten in the drying process.

☼ If you don't wait for the colors to exhaust completely, they will tend to blend in the dyebath and mute each other. Sometimes this is

19

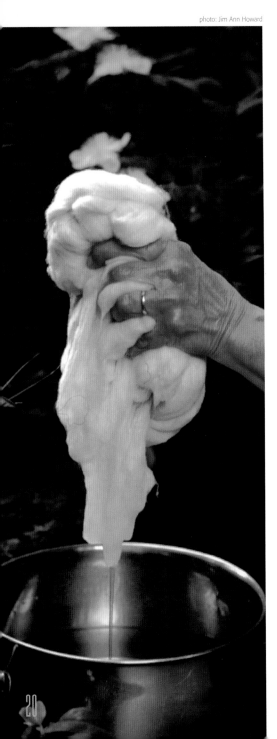

photo: Jim Ann Howard

Grab the entire mass of fiber when lifting wet roving.

desirable and you can let several colors swirl around and blend.

☼ If dye solution takes a long time to exhaust, check the pH of the dyebath. Add more vinegar during dyeing to maintain a constant pH.

☼ It is difficult to see the variations in dark colors when you are working with wet fiber, but they will show up later when the roving is dry.

☼ Know that if you are using dark colors, especially blues and black, the dye will not exhaust completely and the roving will take on an overall cast of these colors. If you want distinctly bright colors on a darker field, then use the cold pour method.

☼ If you let dyed fiber cool in the pan overnight, the colors will be brighter and more washfast. Sometimes dark colors will exhaust completely this way.

☼ Use extra vinegar to lower the pH below 4 to make the dye strike

very quickly if you want the contrast of the white roving against some spots of very strong dots of color.

☼ To superimpose spots of brighter or deeper color onto a roving which is already a light tone, add several pale shades of dye to the dyebath as it heats so the colors diffuse, then add contrasting colors once the dyebath reaches 190°F (88°C).

**COLD POUR DYEING** In this method, you pour dye onto prewetted rovings or

## SUPPLIES FOR COLD POUR DYEING

Newspaper

Good quality plastic wrap

Dye solutions

Easy pouring containers

Trigger-handled spray bottle

Distilled white vinegar

Dyepot with steaming rack

Brick to raise steaming rack in pot
    if necessary

Gloves

▶ When pouring on the dye, begin in the middle of the area you are working with so that the dye has some room to bleed to either side. Pour enough dye to soak in and penetrate to the underside without extra runoff.

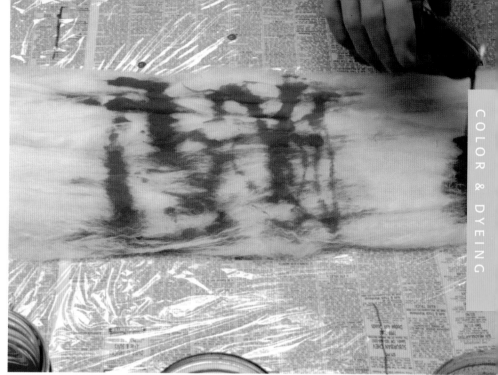

yarn, then wrap the fiber in plastic wrap and steam it to set the dye. This is Twisted Mother Sandy's favorite way to dye. The beauty of this method is that you can prepare and steam several different colored rovings in a relatively short period of time. Depending on the size of your vessel, you can dye up to two pounds (908 g) of fiber at once. You can dye different types of fiber or yarn together or in separate pouches. This technique is very gentle on the fiber and is the best method for dyeing superwash top. The disadvantages are that you really can't tell exactly what the finished product will look like ahead of time, and it is difficult to match anything or reproduce your results. If you dye skeins of yarn this way, there will be a definite repeat pattern.

The following directions are for yard-long (0.91 m) lengths of roving made

▶ Press the dye into the fiber by covering the roving with the plastic and gently "mooshing" it into the fiber mass. This presses the dye through to the underside of the roving before it can run off the sides and helps it travel sideways a bit along the roving. "Sideways mooshing" is also helpful when you want to make adjacent colors blend with each other.

photo: Jim Ann Howard

The finished roving with all dyes applied but not yet wrapped. This was one of the rovings used for the color wheel (see p. 11). The colors from left to right are yellow, yellow-orange, and orange. Dyes that contain yellow will appear somewhat orange until the steaming is complete.

from regular wool, wool blends, and superwash wool. To dye longer pieces of roving, snake it back and forth or coil it onto the plastic so it all fits, using several sheets of plastic overlapped if need be. To dye yarn, work with one skein per piece of plastic. To get more colors on your skein, arrange the yarn in an oval so that there is space in the center of the skein and pour the colors so that each side of the skein is different.

## Procedure

1. Measure or weigh the fiber or yarn you wish to dye and presoak it.
2. Prepare the dye stock solutions and mix your colors.
3. Cover your work surface with newspaper. Tear off a sheet of plastic wrap about 4' (122 cm) long. Lay it nice and flat on the newspaper.
4. Lift a length of roving or a skein of yarn out of the water it has been soaking in and squeeze gently to remove excess water. When lifting

photo: Jim Ann Howard

A plastic packing pillow is inserted under the yellow section of the roving to raise it up. This keeps it from being contaminated by other colors in the same roving during the steaming process.

⚠ When thoroughly heated, well-sealed packets blow up like balloons. This signals that they have been steamed long enough.

roving, fully support the entire mass of fiber in your hands, as wet roving can easily pull apart. The fiber should remain just moist, not wet. (Don't squeeze superwash wool too dry, as it soaks up more liquid than regular wool, and it is harder to get the dye solutions to flow if it is too dry.) Lay the fiber on the plastic wrap.

5. Slowly pour on the dye solution in a steadily controlled stream. By controlling the speed of your pour, you can get the dye to soak into the fiber right where you want it. If you pour on too much dye, it will run and bleed and mute the surrounding colors, and there will be excess dye in the plastic which will drip out when you roll it up to steam. Soak up any excess dye along the sides of the fiber or yarn with dry paper towels before wrapping it up, being careful not to contaminate the colors. Or, lay another piece of wet fiber or yarn on top of the over-saturated area, press gently, and leave it there as you continue. The extra fiber will absorb the excess dye in the steaming process. Continue pouring on colors until the fiber is completely colored to your liking.

6. Spray the fiber with full-strength distilled white vinegar. I use a trigger-handled spray bottle and make sure I squirt each section of the fiber. I have never measured this exactly. You only need to cover the entire surface of the roving with a fine mist. As you squirt it, the vinegar may leave light spots where it has landed on the fiber. Don't worry. The uneven spots and lighter areas of the roving will even out in the steaming process and no vinegar spots will be noticeable.

7. Carefully turn over the fiber by rolling it as a unit. Don't pick it up and let it sag unless you want the colors to run together. If the underside is very pale, you may want to add a little more dye, especially if you want really solid, bright colors. You don't have to spray any vinegar onto this side.

8. Loosely wrap the plastic around the fiber, making sure it overlaps completely and forms a good seal. Don't wrap too snugly, because the liquid inside will expand as it is heated and needs some room to grow. Press any excess dye out the ends onto absorbent paper before you fold the ends over to seal them. Fold the entire packet in thirds or in whatever size will fit into your vessel.

Yellow is easily contaminated by other colors, so if there is any yellow in a roving, put that area on top and slide a plastic packing pillow or a piece of plastic bubble wrap underneath it to keep it raised, after wrapping the roving.

9. Prepare the pot and rack for steaming. Put water 1" (2.5 cm) deep in

Shake spots of color onto the roving.

the bottom of the pot. The rack must be raised at least 3" (7.5 cm) above the water. I set a piece of brick in the pot and put a folding vegetable steamer on top of the brick. Another good setup is a turkey-roasting pan with a raised rack. It's important that the rack be high enough that when the water is simmering and rises in the pan it will not touch the fiber packet, because that can fray or felt the fiber.

Arrange the packets on the rack. Excess dye runs out of the packets and colors the steaming liquid, also raising the liquid level in the vessel. For this reason, when steaming multiple packets, put the darkest colored ones on the bottom with lighter colors on top. This way they won't contaminate each other if a packet happens to pop open during steaming.

10. Bring the vessel to a simmer and steam for 20 minutes. Steaming is complete when the fiber mass is hot all the way through to the center. A good test for this is to lift the lid and find the fiber packet blown up like a balloon.

11. Turn the heat off and let the dyepot cool naturally. If you have the self-control to let it cool overnight before

Press bottle opening onto roving to make larger spots.

▶ Spray roving with vinegar before wrapping and steaming.

photo: Jim Ann Howard

you wash the fiber, you will be well rewarded with brighter, more intense colors and less residual dye.

12. Once the fiber is completely cool, place the packets one at a time in the sink, and wearing gloves, open them carefully. Roll the fiber into the empty sink and discard the plastic. Very gently apply pressure to the fiber to remove excess dye. Wash and rinse the fiber and let it dry.

**SPOT DYEING** This variation on the cold pour technique makes roving or yarn with small dots of color. Arrange presoaked fiber on the plastic wrap. Using a squeeze bottle with a small opening, shake dye solution onto the fiber in a random pattern. To make larger spots, press the bottle opening directly onto the fiber. After applying the dots of color, follow steps 6 through 12 as usual to complete the process and fix the dyes.

Variations for applying color with this technique are endless. Use the same

photo: Jim Ann Howard

▶ These two superwash rovings were dyed with the spot method. The roving on the left was dyed with a lot of large spots. The one on the right was dyed with small spots, widely spaced. The balls of yarn were spun from (top) large spots, (middle) one ply of each, (bottom) small spots. The sock in progress is being knitted with all three yarns, using interrupted rib and Fair Isle stitch patterns.

photo: Jim Ann Howard

Lynne pour-dyed superwash Merino roving with Kool-Aid® colors to make these socks for her niece Holly Jean's twelfth birthday.

dyes all over the fiber for a unified feeling, or use different colors in separate areas for an ever-changing yarn. If you have some blah skeins, overdye them with the spot method. It can give new life to a boring yarn.

**DYEING WITH KOOL-AID®** Kool-Aid® makes a totally nontoxic, washfast dye that is safe and fun for both kids and adults. It's also quick and easy to use. Too bad it doesn't come in more colors!

**Pour-dyeing with Kool-Aid®** Follow the basic directions for hot pour dyeing, substituting Kool-Aid® solutions for the Lanaset® stock solutions.

⚙ To prepare the Kool-Aid® for dyeing, dissolve eight packets unsweetened Kool-Aid® in 1 quart (0.95 l) cold water.

⚙ Pour full-strength Kool-Aid® for intense colors. Dilute it with water for pastels. The colors are intermixable. Try a few drops of Strawberry in ½ cup (120 ml) Lemonade for a cool peach color.

⚙ Fibers and yarn absorb Kool-Aid® colors rapidly, so pour on the solution and soak up excess liquid with a clean sponge before pouring more dye liquid. Repeat until the desired color has been achieved.

**Dip-dyeing with Kool-Aid®, for superwash wool** This is a very quick and easy way to dye. You simply put cold Kool-Aid® in a large glass, plastic, or stainless steel vessel, dip presoaked yarn into the Kool-Aid® to create the color effects you want, then set the dye by steaming. This technique works very well with

superwash wool but gives unpredictable results with plain wool.

As an example, here's how I made the skein shown in this photo. First I soaked the skein until it was thoroughly wet. I then dissolved one packet of Lemon with one-quarter packet of Lime in about 3 cups (720 ml) of cold water in a large vessel. I squeezed most of the water out of the wet skein and quickly pressed it down into the green liquid with my gloved hands. The dye very quickly took up into the skein and the water was clear in no time. I squeezed out the excess liquid and set the skein aside. In this initial dip, the yarn took the dye unevenly—some places were lightly colored, some not at all.

For the frugal at *heart*. Use the residual dye left in the vessel after steaming to DYE FIBER or yarn. This works especially well as an *underdye* for a rich black or dark neutral shade. Just add vinegar to the proper ph of *dyebath* for lanaset or acid dyes, or add MORDANTED WOOL to natural dyes.

— LYNN N'S TIP

Then I mixed one packet of Lime into the 3 cups (720 ml) of water in the vessel. I immersed the skein again, making sure that I turned it so the undyed areas would take the dye first. Once the liquid is squeezed out of the skein, the color stays put and doesn't come off onto surrounding colors. This is an advantage of dyeing with Kool-Aid®. Color placement is fairly easy and much less messy than with other dye methods.

I mixed successive colors to overdye portions of the now light green skein. I used Strawberry and Orange, mixing them one packet to 3 cups (720 ml) water for a pastel shade. For both colors, I dipped a portion of the skein into the dye until it was the color of my liking and squeezed the remaining liquid out of the skein.

Since it takes a stronger solution to overdye an existing color with a deep shade, I mixed the amethyst shade with two packets of Grape in 3 cups (720 ml) water. Again, I dipped in the skein and squeezed out the excess. When I was happy with all the colors on the skein, I sprayed it with white vinegar, wrapped it in plastic wrap, and steamed it as in the cold pour method (see pp. 23–24).

photo: Lynne Vogel

▲ Lynne dip-dyed this 8-ounce (227 g) skein of superwash wool yarn with color from eleven packets of Kool-Aid®.

**To a spinner**, a pile of unspun fiber is utterly irresistible. It is a chance work of art, an abstract composition, a delicacy to the eye and hand. My mom loves to tell a story of her childhood on a cotton plantation and how they would dive into the mountainous pile of cotton as though it were a cloud. I still think of that story when I have a huge pile of fiber on my living room rug. Perhaps I have been unconsciously trying to collect a large enough pile to dive into myself.

Although I dye a lot of my own rovings, I also fall in love and purchase them at fiber fairs. I consider a well-dyed roving to be a "found object"—a thing of beauty in its own right. Each roving is unique, and it is hard enough to reproduce my own successes that I gladly reward another dyer's success by purchasing hers.

But sometimes I fall in love with a beautiful handpainted roving only to find that random spinning doesn't do it justice. This challenges me to find a way to bring out the color a different way.

Careful observation of the colors and their placement and proportion on the roving will open doors to new possibilities. I will talk about how I analyze a roving and how I make the most of quali-ties I wish to enhance. Whether I want the freshness of a singles yarn or the variety of a plied one, taking time to prepare my fiber before spinning makes all the difference in the appearance of the finished yarn.

Although I won't go into the basics of spinning, I will show several different ways to draft color, each method giving a specific effect. There are many ways to spin the same roving. Each person's own hand lends uniqueness to a handspun yarn. This is why we spin in the first place, to feel and see our hands in our work. The addition of a little color makes this even more fun. This chapter holds just a few of the many possibilities of a handpainted roving. Here's hoping you will find new inspiration to enhance your own unique style and method of using color.

## WHAT HAPPENS TO COLORS WHEN YOU SPIN?

It's disappointing to spin a beautiful roving and watch brilliant colors disappear into muddy yarn. It seems as though the more evenly spaced the colors are on a rainbow roving, the duller the yarn becomes.

Size and optical mixing are the culprits. Spinning reduces the color to a thin line. Then in the twisting that occurs in plying, the lines are broken into dots. The eye automatically mixes these lines or dots of adjacent colors, producing a third color. For instance, orange and turquoise make a muddy color when mixed together. (They are called complementary colors for this reason.) Orange and turquoise plied together look muddy from a distance, even though they still appear orange and turquoise up close. When a roving contains many pairs of complements, such as red and green, orange and blue, yellow and violet, each time these colors come adjacent to each other in plying or knitting, they dull each other.

Muddy-looking yarn is not always the inevitable outcome of a rainbow roving. The trick is to separate the colors so that larger areas of them are visible, just like they appear in the unspun roving. One way of separating the colors or groups of colors is to do so before spinning.

To SPIN solid *colors* from a multicolored roving, make sure that the *color bands* are longer than the average fiber length.

—DEBBIE'S TIP

Sandy dyed her Crayons color combination on this Blue-faced Leicester roving, which has an average staple length of over 4 inches (10 cm). The colors are dyed in crisply defined bands 6 inches (15 cm) or longer. The yarn in the center was randomly spun from this roving.

Laying out strips of prepared roving will give you some control over your color sequences. Plying like tones with like will make the colors look fresher when spinning a two-ply yarn. Navajo plying will keep solid colors in sequence rather than breaking them up in the plying process.

photo: Jim Ann Howard

**Look it over first** Before I start to spin a roving, I like to lay it out and take a good look at it. This gives me a chance to admire the colors and the fiber, and I enjoy doing this even if my intention is to spin it randomly just for the joy of spinning. But sometimes I have a special project in mind or I want a certain effect from the colors. Then I examine the roving more closely. While it is true that I can never be sure exactly how a yarn will look until it is spun, considering the following points helps give me an idea of what to expect. With thought and preparation and a unique approach, it is possible to get a lot out of a length of multicolored fiber.

⌘ Staple length and color banding. I pull a few fibers out of the roving in several places, measure the

staple, or fiber length, and compare that with the average length of the color bands. If the color bands are longer than the average staple length, the colors will spin up pure and clean with a smooth gradation between colors. In this case, you have the option of pulling apart the different colors and spinning them separately. But if the color bands are shorter than the staple length, the colors will blend with each other in spinning and only very short lengths of the pure color will appear in the yarn. The yarn spun from the spotted roving shown on p. 25 is a perfect example of this. All the colors blend throughout the yarn in a random and unpredictable way,

and there are very few pure white or deeply colored areas.

⌘ Proportion of colors. In the Crayons roving, most of the colors of the rainbow are present. It is reasonable to predict that when this roving is randomly spun and plied onto itself each color will meet up with itself and each of the other colors at intervals. Even though it appears to be a brilliantly contrasting multi-colored yarn, most of the colors are yellow, orange, and red, and the yarn has a decidedly orange overall effect from a distance.

By comparison, the second Tide Pool roving on p. 13 is a good illustration of a color combination with a dominant hue. Since it is mostly a muted aqua with

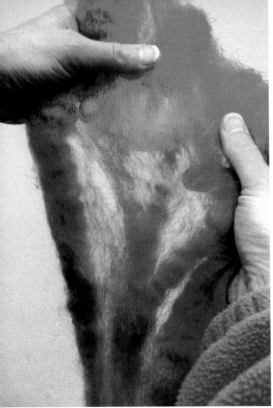

◀ Fluff by gently opening the roving 1 foot (30.5 cm) at a time.

photo: Lynne Vogel

sider using it for a singles yarn. Shorter, finer fibers such as Merino or cashmere lend themselves wonderfully to plied yarns.

**FIBER PREPARATION** Taking the time to prepare a roving well pays off in spinning pleasure and in the appearance of the finished yarn. "Fluffing" the fiber lets you get a feel for how it drafts before you decide how to spin it. Ideas often occur to me in the fiber preparation stage because the feel of a fiber tells me much more than its appearance.

By separating and splitting the roving I can create desired color effects. Sometimes I recombine the divided roving in new ways before spinning. Occasionally I even card the dyed fiber to blend the colors. Depending on how

I prepare it before I spin, the same roving can make many different yarns.

**Fluffing the fibers** First I "fluff" the whole length of the roving to gently separate the fibers and make the dividing process easier. If I have dyed the roving myself, I will do some of this fluffing as the roving is drying to speed the drying time.

Fluffing helps coax any tangled fibers to release their grip on each other without tearing the roving apart. It gives me a chance to evaluate the hand of the fiber, to loosen any felting that has occurred in the dyeing process, to examine more closely the staple length and draftability of the fiber, and to begin designing the yarn. For example, if short, soft wool such as Merino has felted in the least bit, it

short intervals of other colors, the yarn looks aqua with accent colors for character. No matter how you spin it, the overall effect will be the same.

∞ Repeat pattern. There is a definite repeat pattern in the Crayons roving: yellow, green, yellow, orange, red, violet, red, orange. Depending on how I proceed with a roving like that, I can use the repeat pattern to achieve certain effects.

∞ Fiber type. If the roving is a strong, long-staple wool like Blue-faced Leicester or Wensleydale, I con-

▶ Gently tug at a diagonal to realign the fibers. I call this "making the state of Tennessee."

photo: Lynne Vogel

photo: Lynne Vogel

becomes difficult to draft into a smooth, fine yarn, but a roving like that can still make a nice textured or fluffy yarn.

Once I have fluffed the entire length, I then split the roving into manageable sections for spinning. There are several ways to do this.

**Separating crosswise** If I want to separate the colors and spin solid yarns, I pull the roving apart crosswise in chunks of solid colors. This is only possible if the bands of color are longer than the staple length of the fiber; otherwise, I can't fully separate the chunks from the adjacent colors.

I often want a bit of the neighboring color to show up in my solid because it gives the yarn character and coordinates it with other yarns spun from the same roving, so I separate the roving right at the junction of two colors. When I spin this piece from the fold, small bits of the contrasting colors at both ends of the solid chunk will wander randomly into the yarn, giving it a subtly heathered look.

But if I want a totally pure color, I separate the color I want about an inch or two from the neighboring color so that no strands of that other color will compromise its clarity. Doing this makes some leftovers, but I can always use them somehow. There's less waste if the roving has long (a foot [30.5 cm] or so) sections of pure colors.

After separating a roving crosswise, I spin the chunks from the fold for a smooth yarn. This technique is good for making long lengths of a single color within a yarn. A singles spun in this manner is especially desirable for Navajo plying.

◀ After splitting a roving crosswise, you can spin the chunks from the fold. This makes a smooth, solid-color singles yarn or a slightly heathered yarn, depending on where the roving was split in the color sequence.

*Hummingbird handspindle from Woolly Designs.*

◀ By pulling apart areas that are dyed different colors, you can use parts of a roving to spin solid-color yarns. Since this split is right on the junction between the two colors, fibers of both colors are present on each side of the split.

**Splitting lengthwise** If I want the lengths of colors in my yarn to change at short intervals, I split the roving into long narrow strips by halving the entire piece, then halving it again and so on until I have a number of thin strands. The thinner the strand, the shorter the color band in the spun yarn. Lengthwise splitting works especially well for spinning on the drop spindle, as I can wind the narrow strand around my wrist and spin away. Beginning spinners can use this technique to good advantage because narrow strips minimize the need for drafting. A strip like this can be spun into a

photo: Lynne Vogel

FROM FIBER TO YARN

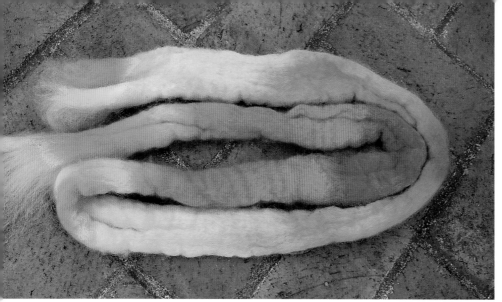

photo: Lynne Vogel

 If a roving has a definite repeat, pull it apart at the repeat points. The roving shown here has several repeats. By dividing the yellow, green, yellow section from the orange, red, violet section, you can spin two entirely different yarns.

lovely thick and thin singles with no drafting at all, another technique for the beginning drop spindler.

**Organizing repeats** To make the most from a repeat pattern, I choose a point in the repeat and pull apart the roving at each of these points, dividing it into chunks as long as the repeat. Then I organize these chunks so the repeats all go in the same direction, either by laying them side by side or by coiling them and putting them in a box or basket.

**Organizing plies** One of my favorite color techniques is plying different colorways together. To get an idea of what two different rovings might look like plied together, I simply twist the two rovings

together and squint my eyes to imagine that large twist as a small yarn. I can actually determine what colors will ply with others by separating thin strips and laying them side by side. If the strips are the same length and thickness, the yarns spun from them will be roughly the

photo: Lynne Vogel

same. This is never entirely accurate, but it helps keep colors in the neighborhood of where I want them.

**Combination drafting** A wonderful tweed effect can be had by drafting several different colorways together at once. This gives a singles yarn a plied look and a plied yarn a very tweedy, blended look. It helps to evenly distribute colors through a yarn, to break stripes into a more random pattern, or to blend contrasting colors into a more homogenous whole. The possibilities are endless.

Twisting two rovings helps you preview a color combination, so you can decide if you want to spin those rovings and ply the yarns together.

▶ Use combination drafting to create a tweed effect. Lay thin strips of roving side by side so different colors line up. These are strips from the same roving, with contrasting colors side by side. Hold the combination of strips and gently predraft them as a unit to prepare the fiber for spinning.

Take two or more thin strips of roving of different colors and lay them side by side lengthwise. They can be strips of the same roving laid in opposite directions so that contrasting colors line up, or strips from different rovings. Gently predraft the strips as a unit to make the fibers mingle with one another and form one thin strand. They will draft more smoothly if the fiber content of the rovings is the same, but interesting textural effects can come from combining different fibers in this manner. Predrafting is a wonderful technique for the drop spindle. I find that it speeds up the process of spinning and also makes it more enjoyable.

**Carding** Sometimes I just don't like the colors in a roving, or I want them to be more homogenized. Or I might want to add another fiber such as angora to the wool. Sandy has a huge commercial carding machine that makes a roving or a batt with equal ease. She runs a roving through with a bit of brightly colored angora and out comes a blurred version

▶ Blending colors by carding them together can result in a beautiful heathered yarn. Other fibers, such as bits of silk, can be added for a textured yarn.

photo: Lynne Vogel

photo: Lynne Vogel

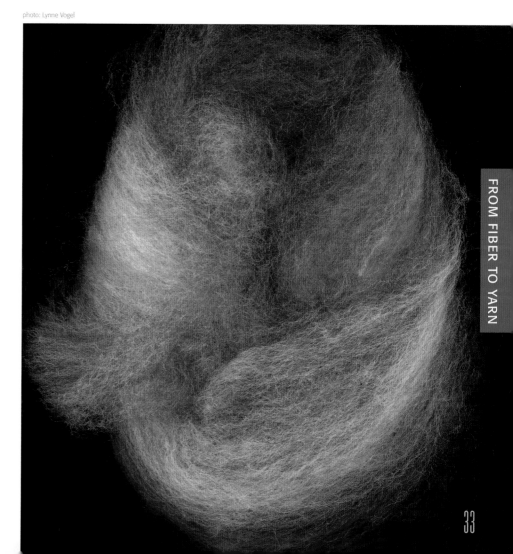

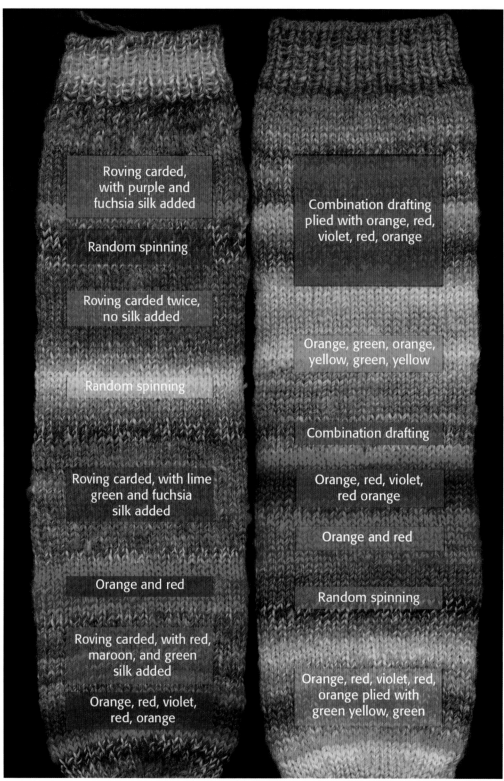

Roving carded,
with purple and
fuchsia silk added

Random spinning

Roving carded twice,
no silk added

Random spinning

Roving carded, with lime
green and fuchsia
silk added

Orange and red

Roving carded, with red,
maroon, and green
silk added

Orange, red, violet,
red, orange

Combination drafting
plied with orange, red,
violet, red, orange

Orange, green, orange,
yellow, green, yellow

Combination drafting

Orange, red, violet,
red orange

Orange and red

Random spinning

Orange, red, violet, red,
orange plied with
green yellow, green

▶ These tubes include all the yarns discussed in this section. All yarns are two-ply, starting with the Crayons roving. The labels identify how the colors were used in the singles. Except where noted, the singles yarn was plied with itself.

photo: Lynne Vogel

of the roving with warm, fuzzy speckles. I like to blend a roving on my drumcarder and include bits of cut silk or mohair locks to add interest. Either way, the yarns are more subdued and the socks quieter. Some days I need quiet socks.

## THE SPINDLE AND THE SOCK ADDICT'S SURVIVAL KIT

The spindle is one of the most ancient tools known to humans. Whenever I feel the need to connect with my basic inner being I pick one up and begin to spin. The sense of calm that envelops me is almost immediate. Automatically I focus on the feel of the twist, the slow pull of the fibers as I draft, the quiet hum of the whorl as I give it another good twirl. I love to admire the finished yarn as I wind it

▶ These are my first spindle socks. I spun all the yarn while we were moving cross-country. I used two different colored Merino rovings, plying them with themselves and each other to make three coordinated yarns. I had a fairly short spindle and could spin in the cab of the truck while James drove through state after state. Memories of the May twilight in Missouri coming through the windshield onto the warm tones in my yarn are still fresh in my mind.

**ORGANIZING TIP**

When organizing lengths of roving for spinning, you can initially join two lengths by overlapping the ends and gently pre-drafting them. This makes the fibers friendly enough for those ends to cling together when gently handled. This way you can coil several lengths around your wrist for drop spindling. ⊠

photo: Lynne Vogel

FROM FIBER TO YARN

Never be without your current sock project. Here's all you need to take your spinning and knitting with you everywhere. I like to carry my knitting in a shoulder bag or fanny pack; that way I can knit while standing in a long line. The bag keeps my yarn from rolling away.

**MUST HAVES:**

Spindle

8 ounces (227 g) of fiber

Your choice of knitting needles

Darning needle

Scissors

6" (15 cm) ruler

A pattern (probably
   memorized or on a
   card jn knitter's
   shorthand)

Eyeglasses, if necessary

A bag to hold it all

**OPTIONAL AND SOMETIMES
NECESSARY TOYS:**

Itty-bitty niddy-noddy

Felt balls on which to wind yarn

Nøstepinne

Needle case to hold darning needles

A *beautiful* bag to hold it all

▶ Since I like to spin
way out in the woods, I
carry my spinning in true
survival-kit fashion.

photo: Lynne Vogel

onto the shaft. Truly this is medicine for the soul.

The spindle has been a patient teacher and a good companion. I don't think I could have ever learned to spin if it hadn't been for this tool. I had tried spinning on different wheels many times, but found them to be demons of frustration. Because I could go slowly enough with the drop spindle to get a handle on the proper feeling of twist and the smooth pull of successful drafting, I finally crossed the threshold into the world of the spinner. What a magical time that was. I spun on my spindle every day and dreamt about it every night. All of a sudden I lived to spin. Why had I waited so long to learn? I spun everything I could get my hands on, and within a month I was borrowing a wheel and making peace with the monster. After so many attempts, I was finally spinning.

Even though I now feel comfortable at a wheel, I still appreciate a spindle. Every time I return to it I learn some new finesse that I can take back to the wheel. On the spindle I slow down and focus. It gives me the time to practice a different fiber or technique. Then I take my new skills to the wheel and perfect them there as well. When I return to the spindle, the cycle repeats itself.

Because the spindle is so portable, I use it to spin on long trips, in the woods, or in other places I can't easily take a wheel. Whereas it might be daunting to spin enough for a large pullover, making yarn for a project like socks is quickly accomplished with a drop spindle. It's especially handy for spinning small amounts of many colors; it is an indispensable creative tool.

**DESIGNING TWO-PLY YARNS** Most of the time I make two-ply yarns for socks, and combining colors in two-ply yarns is one of my favorite things to do. I could do this day in and day out.

It's fun and easy to grab a bag of handpainted roving, spin it, and ply it onto itself, and there will be plenty of variegations in this randomly spun and plied yarn. But that's only the tip of a huge iceberg. Very often, plying singles spun from different rovings gives even more wonderful results.

From two different rovings, you can make three different two-ply yarns; two that are plied on themselves and another that has one strand of each plied together (see socks on p. 35). One of my very favorite ways to use hand-painted rovings is to choose at least three or four different rovings and combine them in as many two-ply yarns as possible. Three rovings will make up to six different yarns, all of which are related to each other. Four rovings can make as many as ten different yarns!

Usually, I simply ply the different colors together in several different combinations and change yarns as I knit. It is possible, though, to keep varying colors in the spinning process by joining a sequence of rovings in a singles yarn. Overlap the different rovings at a similar color so that the join segues from one to the next. Joining the rovings in a random fashion so that the colors combine in unexpected ways when plied makes a continuously changing and unpredictable yarn that is an endless pleasure to knit.

## Combining colors in two-ply yarns

Contrasting colors give a combination a tweed or speckled look, while like colors look calm and coordinated. Finding the right balance is often a matter of taste and experimentation, but understanding the basic qualities of color (see p. 8) and the types of color contrast can help you decide. Although the socks illustrated here

> To test *lightness* (value) of colored yarns, copy them on a BLACK AND WHITE photo copy machine. If they are of similar value, they will be a similar *shade of gray* in the copy (see pp. 8 and 38).
>
> —LYNNE'S TIP

contain many colors, most of them are fairly similar in value and saturation. They vary more in hue.

Drawing from natural color combinations is one way to learn effective color use. I studied the zinnias in my garden as a good example of brilliant colors in combination. Most of the flowers were red, orange, and violet, vivid warm tones, with only a few pink and lavender blooms. No matter what color the flower was, though, the back of the petals was a light, fresh mint green that would peek around from the underside of the petal as the flower opened. In my combination, I chose to dye predominantly warm and vivid colors with only a few muted shades added to suggest shadows. To make this combination truly reminiscent of zinnias, I added a few small sections of mint green in the roving. (I actually used three different, closely-related greens: a light mint, a little darker mint,

◀ The Zinnias socks.

and a yellow-green as pale as the lighter mint. Because I used the greens sparingly, they don't overpower and thereby dull the warmer tones, but suggest an accent of leaves and sunlight.)

The Zinnias socks illustrate three kinds of contrast:

∞ Variation of lightness (value): Most of the colors are on the darker side of medium range, with a few light and dark shades.

∞ Variation of color (hue): Most of the colors are warm tones between orange and violet on the color wheel, with a few cool greens from the opposite side of the wheel.

∞ Variation of brightness (saturation): Most of the colors are brilliant. Only a few are dull.

The Autumn Flowers socks are another example of color combinations inspired by nature.

A field of wildflowers flanks a nearby lake. All year long I find glorious color combinations here, but my favorite time to view them is autumn. The brightly colored flowers and leaves hold their heads

◀ The Autumn Flowers socks.

Here's a look inside the Zinnias (right) and Autumn Flowers (left) socks. I used these eight rovings and combined them into various two-ply yarns. The letters next to the socks show which roving I combined for each yarn.

A. Zinnias roving: red, violet, orange, mint green, lavender

B. Vermillion blend roving: orange red (vermillion), cherry red, blood red, darker mint, yellow-green

C. Sandy's Wine Country roving: Bordeaux, eggplant, medium violet, muted teal (just a bit)

D. Violet blend roving: violet, deep violet, medium lavender

E. Autumn leaves roving: muted pastel shades of pumpkin and coral pink, russet brown, apricot, light olive green, light blue gray

F. Mustard blend roving: mustard olive, burnt sienna, soft gold

G. Mango blend roving: mango wool blended with mohair dyed lime green, orange, and brown

H. Madder blend roving: shades of wool dyed with madder (a plant dye) blended with mohair dyed green, aqua, and hot pink

photo: Lynne Vogel

# Autumn in the Fields

Crimson sumac branches flaunt

their drooping fruits to *the sun*.

Dusty and waiting for rain,

they mimic clusters OF RUBIES

in dried blood. Their *garnet* leaves

are heavily spotted with UMBER

remnants of a rainy summer.

Leaf stems *glowing* in currant jelly,

the same leaves' undersides

are chocolate spotted spring green,

washed with sheer *watermelon*.

Green carpet beneath lifts each warm tone

skyward into clicking, buzzing

GRASSHOPPER song and seeds

of tall *purple* grass that brushes

my shoulders as I pass.

above the dying grasses in an infinitely rich display. I started by dyeing an autumn leaves combination in muted shades of pumpkin, coral pink, russet brown, apricot, light olive green, and light blue gray. It wasn't too surprising to find that I already had some other rovings around that coordinated with this one.

Most colors in this combination are of medium saturation, muted but not dull. They are mostly of medium to light-medium value, overall a bit lighter than the ones in the Zinnias socks. As in the Zinnias socks, most of the color variation is in hue.

Although one roving (Sandy's Wine Country combination) was used in both socks, it looks different because I plied it with brilliant colors that are the same light value for the Zinnias socks, and with more muted colors for the Autumn Leaves socks.

**WORKING WITH SINGLES** I got inspired to work with singles by studying with Kathryn Alexander. She is an innovative spinner and knitter who teaches

▶ Spin a singles with just enough twist that it plies back onto itself to make a soft two-ply yarn like this.

a stimulating class on using energized singles yarns. With a lot of hard work and experimentation she has developed creative ways of featuring the bias that occurs with singles. Her work is astonishingly fresh and unique because her yarns are fresh. Yes, fresh off the bobbin, with no finishing.

After taking her class I tried some of these techniques and found that my favorite way to use fresh yarn was right off a spindle. The next time I had a full spindle of yarn, instead of plying it as usual, I cast on some stitches and began knitting in garter stitch, unrolling the yarn directly off the spindle as I went along. Immediately falling in love with the fabric, I spun some more, knitted some more, and my knitted panel grew. I loved

photo: Lynne Vogel

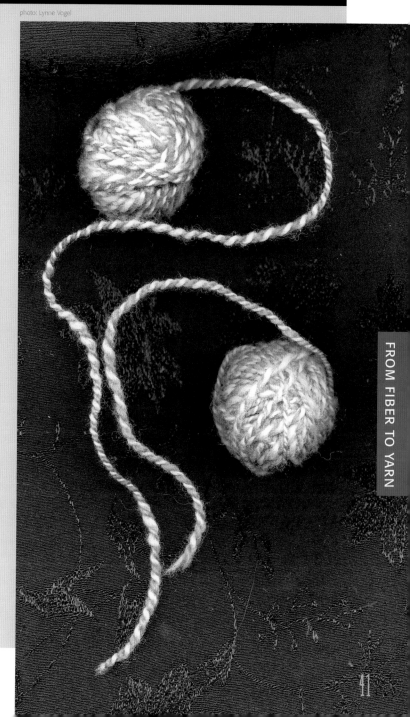

photo: Lynne Vogel

Working with variegated yarns is very much like painting with yarn. There is so much color detail that is an integral part of each strand that echoes the myriad colors in nature. Just knitting with these yarns is a delicious experience.

A favorite technique of mine is to segue from one yarn to the next by changing yarns at a point in each where they are very similar if not exact. For instance, as I am knitting along I may come to a point where my two-ply yarn has one ply of pale mauve and one of white. Then I look to see if there is another ball in my basket that has a different combination of colors that also contains pale mauve and white and begins with a pale mauve/white ply combination. If I choose this ball to work with, I tie it on and continue knitting. Sometimes I run out of yarn, and to match the end I have to wind a bit off another ball. That may seem wasteful, but every bit of yarn ends up in the perfect place at one time or another, so I wind off what I need and save the rest for another day. I use this technique with singles as well.

▶ When joining on a new yarn, overlap the ends at a place where the same color combination occurs.

FROM FIBER TO YARN

41

how portable this process was and kept on going to make a vest. The stitches had a pearly quality that my finished singles don't have and the fabric has a lively feel, unlike some garter stitch fabric, which can be very stiff. I realized that I had used just the very basics of Kathryn's technique to make a simple piece I never grow tired of wearing.

I soon found that energized singles make wonderful sock yarns. Singles yarns resemble the original roving more than any other yarn. This keeps the colors fresh and exciting. The fabric is light, resilient, comfortable to wear, and remarkably durable and beautiful. I love spinning on the drop spindle and immediately knitting the yarn without plying or finishing of any kind.

**Guidelines on using singles** There are a few rules to follow when using energized singles yarns. The very basics

Ply VARIEGATED singles with textured ones spun from *curly mohair* or angora for luxurious novelty yarns.

—SANDY'S TIP

▲ Debby spun Blue-faced Leicester roving with more twist than usual and knitted the singles yarn on large needles to make this enchanting leg warmer. It has a ruffled cast on and tapers gently from the knee to the ankle. The fabric is remarkably light, stretchy, and alive.

◀ This sock was knitted entirely from energized singles spun on the drop spindle. Garter stitch mosaic bands alternate with stockinette bands of S- and Z-twist yarns. The heel and toe are knitted from two strands at a time, one S and one Z. Notice that the only areas that slant are the stockinette bands. The rest of the sock is straight-grained.

▶ This simple sock was spun from a Blue-faced Leicester roving and knitted fresh from the spindle. It has a picot cast on and a k1, p1 rib. Most of the sock is worked in stockinette stitch, but to make the heel straight-grained I worked it plus a few rows before and after it in seed stitch. The sock is finished with a round toe. Since a round toe doesn't have to align with the heel, you can start the decreases at any point on the round and the toe will fit perfectly.

FROM FIBER TO YARN

photo: Lynne Vogel

Treasure bags made from energized singles are especially fun because they are small, fast, portable projects. For this treasure bag, I spun two S-twist energized singles. The brilliant bands are from Sandy's Blue-faced Leicester Crayons roving, and the more autumnal tones are from some pour-dyed alpaca fleece. I started at the top with a stretchy cast on (see p. 68), then worked several rows of k1, p1 ribbing. To make holes for the drawstring, I worked a series of *k2tog, yo* near the top of the bag. The body of the bag is stockinette stitch. At the bottom of the bag, I used the two yarns alternately in Fair Isle technique. To finish off, I worked k2tog for one round to decrease, worked eight more rounds, then ran the yarn through the remaining stitches. For the drawstring, I made two tightly twisted two-ply yarns, then let them double back on themselves, and threaded them through the holes.

▶ Lynne knitted this colorful bag from energized singles yarns.

44

are as follows. For more complete instructions on how to use an energized singles yarn, please refer to Kathryn Alexander's article in *SpinOff* Spring 2002, (pp. 54–61).

- Try to spin a fairly consistent singles yarn with just enough twist that it plies back onto itself to make a soft two-ply yarn. Too little twist and you won't get the desired stitch tilt definition in your fabric. (The photos here show ideal stitch tilt; aim for something like that.) With too much twist, your fabric will be kinky and uneven.

- Long-staple wools are typically coarser than short-staple wools and have enough body to create extra stitch definition. In addition to slanting, one side of each stitch comes forward and becomes prominent. This creates a very attractive shibori-like effect. Among the long-staple wools, I think Blue-faced Leicester is the softest and most comfortable to wear.

- Spin only what you can knit within a few days. If it sits on the

bobbin or spindle too long, the yarn relaxes and becomes unpredictable to work with.

- Knit the yarn by unrolling it off the spindle or bobbin. Don't wind it into a ball or let it come off the end of the shaft of the spindle.

- The yarn will twist back onto itself as you knit. This takes some getting used to, but before long, handling it will become familiar.

- Secure the yarn ends right away. Weave them into the fabric or crochet a chain with the cast-on tail to use for finishing later.

- Using garter, moss, or seed stitch, ribbing, or any equal combination of knits and purls (such as k2, p2 ribbing or knit 2 rows, purl 2 rows) produces a straight-grained fabric. All other stitch patterns will slant.

- Knitting stockinette stitch in the round creates a wonderful spiral effect that is continuous because there are no seams or selvedges to worry with. Just knit, knit, knit. To make a tube sock, just cast on the appropriate number of stitches, work a few inches of ribbing,

then knit in stockinette to your desired length. Finish with a round toe (see p. 80).

- Spinning singles in both directions, S and Z, opens the door to more options. Knit a beautiful fabric by knitting two strands of energized singles together at the same time. Knit one S and one Z to balance out any slant that would occur from using either one alone. This forms a straight-grained fabric that has subtle depth and wonderful strength. The difference from a plied yarn is subtle and indescribable. The two strands seem to repel each other, giving a certain life to the fabric. This fabric is much more durable than it might seem.

- Knitting stockinette stitch in the round with S and Z yarns alternately in any combination makes a zigzag pattern. For instance, knit six rows S and six rows Z. Since you are knitting in the round, there is no irregular selvedge to worry about. Knit the heel and possibly the toe of the sock with S and Z combined, as above.

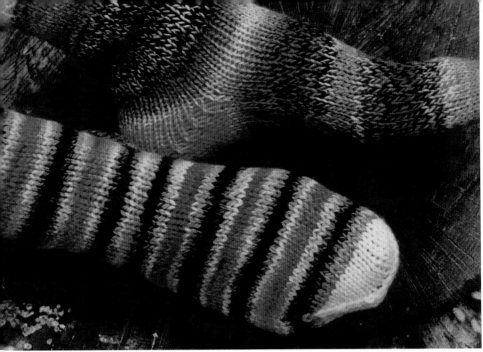

Alina combines two-ply and Navajo-ply yarns in her socks, using roving that Sandy dyed in shades of yellow, orange, lime green, and black. Top: This sock uses both multicolor and solid-color two-ply yarns. Bottom: The yarn in this sock was Navajo-plied from the same roving.

photo: Jim Ann Howard

## MAKING NAVAJO THREE-PLY YARNS

Although many spinners, including some of the Twisted Sisters, believe that three-ply yarns are the ultimate sock yarns, I usually prefer two-ply and singles yarns myself. I don't like how plying from three bobbins homogenizes the colors.

But sometimes I use the Navajo plying technique, because it combines the color qualities of a singles yarn with the durability and practicality of a plied one. If you don't know how to Navajo-ply, ask a spinning friend to teach you. It's a won-

photo: Jim Ann Howard

Alina combined multicolor and solid-color two-ply yarns with Navajo-ply yarns in this whimsical pair.

derful technique to know, especially if you want a yarn that changes endlessly from one solid color to the next. Navajo plying combines the color qualities of a singles yarn with the durability and practicality of a plied one. Although it is difficult to beat a singles yarn for truly crisp and clear colors, a plied yarn is often more practical for socks. Navajo plying, with its series of sequential loops, makes a three-ply yarn directly from one singles and maintains the original color sequence of the singles yarn.

▶ Debby dyed, spun, and Navajo-plied her two favorite colorways, then knit these beauties with Fair Isle technique. She achieved a fascinating effect with continously flowing color sequences without constantly having to change her yarns to make those color changes.

photo: Jim Ann Howard

# Knitting
# SOCKS

**Why knit socks?** In this day and age it might seem as though it takes a lot of time and effort to knit a pair of socks. And while a sweater lasts for years and years, socks may not last very long without wearing through in places. Why spend so much time on something that won't last?

Besides, how will they fit? They might be like those awful little socks I had to wear as a kid that bunched into my shoes, were too tight or too loose, and made my life miserable. Not to mention that I'd have to use those pointy needles. These are the reasons I used for avoiding sock knitting. I'm sure you have a list of your own.

But, I really did love the socks my friends were knitting. They were soft and colorful, they used very little yarn, and they knitted up in no time. I noticed that Sandy, especially, never wore anything but Birkenstocks. There isn't enough shoe area on a Birkenstock to wear out a sock. And the sock shows. You can admire your work while wearing it.

This caused me to reconsider. It occurred to me that I would spin yarn for socks that I wouldn't use for a sweater. Since I thrive on variety, this seemed very appealing.

Every now and then Sandy would hand me one of her space-dyed rovings, an unpopular blend or just a boo-boo and say, "Do you like this?" I would invariably say, "Yes, I love it." "Well then, it's yours," she would reply.

Gradually I acquired a bunch of these beauties. Sorting through my stash, I found a burgundy and forest combination in wool and a maroon, burgundy, and charcoal combination in a rayon/Merino blend. I spun the two rovings and plied the yarns together. The colors enhanced each other and looked much better plied to each other than plied to themselves. As I knitted the socks, I enjoyed the tiny dots of color in each stitch, the constant change of shade that passed through my fingers. Unwittingly I made mistakes here and there—cuffs too loose, heel too shallow, foot too wide. After a few wearings, I purposefully felted them. They fit a bit better. In wearing them though, even with their flaws, I noticed that they had a life that was missing from my store-bought socks. I liked them so much I decided to try again.

As I became passionate about sock knitting, I began knitting tubes of color as sample swatches. The tubes were the same size as regular socks, so I could turn the swatches into socks

*Mistakes* can be design **opportunities**. Blunders often introduce a different perspective from which to develop a *unique style*.

—LYNNE'S TIP

when I liked the sample. I wish I had knitted all my sample swatches like this. Imagine all the great socks that would have come from them.

Knitters who have never made a sock before will find fun things to do in this chapter. I'll start with a basic pattern and will show you how to abbreviate

▶ Twisted Sisters make a wonderful variety of socks. Clockwise from center bottom: Lynne's curly mohair sock, Debby's legwarmer, Linda's Merino/Tencel® sock, Linda's back-and-forth sock, Lynne's Zinnia, Lynne's mosaic, Lynne's back-and-forth, Sandy's loop mohair, Sandy's knock-your-socks-off sock, Lynne's spindle sock.

| | |
|---|---|
| BN | blunt tapestry needle |
| BO | bind off |
| CN | circular needle |
| CO | cast on |
| dec(s) | decrease(s) |
| dp | double-pointed |
| inc | increase(s) |
| k | knit |
| k tbl | knit through back loop |
| k2tog | knit two stitches together |
| kwise | knitwise |
| M1 | make one stitch |
| N1 | first needle |
| p | purl |
| psso | pass slipped stitch over |
| p2tog | purl two stitches together |
| pwise | purlwise |
| rem | remaining |
| rep | repeat |
| rnd(s) | round(s) |
| RS | right side |
| sl | slip |
| spi | stitches per inch |
| ssk | slip, slip, knit 2 sl sts tog |
| st(s) | stitch(es) |
| St st | stockinette stitch |
| tog | together |
| wpi | wraps per inch |
| WS | wrong side |
| wyb | with yarn in back |
| wyf | with yarn in front |
| yo | yarn over |
| * | repeat starting point (i.e., repeat from *) |
| ** | repeat all instructions between asterisks |

the pattern for quick reference. Beyond that, my purpose is to show you how to design socks, not just follow patterns. I'll explain how to think of a sock as a group of design elements, such as heels and toes. I'll also show several ways to knit tubes and how to reassemble different elements to form custom sock patterns of your own.

**A BASIC SOCK PATTERN** Here's a versatile basic pattern. It has a very elastic cast on or bind off for a non-binding cuff. The leg and foot are mostly stockinette stitch so there is plenty of room for adding stitch patterns or showing off pretty yarns. The hourglass heel and the wedge toe can be knitted cuff down or toe up. It is broken down into elements, so that you may substitute other elements from this book or your own favorites.

**Size:** Women's medium (about 8½" [21.5 cm] around foot). Foot length to be determined by the individual knitter.

▶ This basic sock is knitted with Henry's Attic Kona Superwash Merino yarn dyed with the cold pour spot method.

Medium-sized feet are typically 8½" to 10" (21.5 to 25.5 cm) long.

**Yarn:** Light worsted-weight wool, approximately 12 to 13 wraps per inch (wpi). About 5 ounces (142 g) or 325 yards (297 m) for one pair of socks.

**Gauge:** 26 sts = 4" (10 cm) in stockinette st. I measure length in inches, not rounds, so I don't figure row gauge. I do count rows after I knit the first sock, so I can duplicate it exactly for the second one of the pair.

**Needles:** Size 3 (3.25 mm) or size needed to obtain gauge double-pointed, set of five.

**Working sts:** 56.

**Elements:** This pattern can be worked from the cuff down or from the toe up.

photo: Lynne Vogel

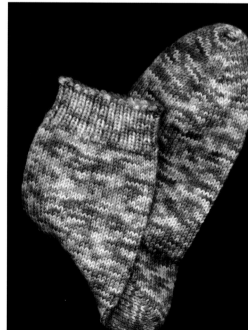

Either way, it includes the same elements:

- ❖ Cast on, or bind off: Stretchy cast on for cuff down. If worked toe up, finish the cuff with an invisible bind off (p. 70). Both are very elastic.
- ❖ Cuff: K1, p1 ribbing.
- ❖ Leg: Stockinette, the perfect canvas for colorwork.
- ❖ Heel: Hourglass heel; it fits comfortably and works the same from either direction.
- ❖ Foot: Stockinette.
- ❖ Toe: Wedge toe; it fits snugly and keeps the sock from twisting on the foot.

**Note:** In these directions, I refer to needles by number. Needle one (N1) is the needle I first knit from after joining the round. The point where N1 and N4 join is the center back of the leg and bottom of the foot. I leave the cast-on tail to mark this juncture; it signals the beginning of each round.

### Knitting the sock cuff down

**Top edge** CO 112 sts with loop cast on. Transfer 28 sts to each of four needles. (I prefer to cast onto a regular long needle, then knit off onto four dp needles.) Being careful not to twist the row, join the round.

*Rnd 1:* *Ssk, p2tog* around (56 sts), or cast on 56 sts in long tail cast on (p.68).

**Cuff:** Work k1, p1 ribbing until the cuff measures 1½" (3.8 cm) long or desired length.

**Leg:** Knit until leg (not including cuff) measures 4" (10 cm), or desired length to measure 2" (5 cm) above bottom of heel. Knit to the end of N3 and stop. (If I want to change colors for the heel, I do it here. If I want the body of the sock to continue in the color I have used up to this point, I don't break the yarn, but drop it and pick it up when mentioned later.)

### Begin the heel

*Row 1 (RS):* Knit all the sts from N4 and N1 onto one needle and turn–28 sts. You are now ready to knit back and forth. (At this point I like to put the sts from N2 and N3 onto waste yarn, because if I don't do that, I pull the sts at the corner of the heel every time I turn the row and it leaves a large st which looks like a hole when I continue knitting the instep.)

*Row 2 (WS):* Yo pwise, p28.

*Row 3:* Yo kwise, knit across to the last 2 sts and turn, leaving those 2 sts on

photo: Lynne Vogel

the left needle. They will look like a tight pair.

Continue in this manner. On each successive row, begin with a yo and purl or knit up to a tight pair and turn. This leaves an increasing number of pairs on the needles. When you finish the ninth pair on the right side row, purl back and prepare to turn the heel.

### Turn the heel

*Row 1 (RS):* Yo, knit across to the first pair and knit the first st of the pair, turn.

*Row 2 (WS):* Yo, purl across to the first pair and purl the first st of the pair, turn.

*Row 3 (RS):* Yo, knit across to the yo from the previous row. There will be 2 yo's on the left needle, then a row of pairs. Slip the 2 yo's and the first st of the next pair kwise and return them to the left needle. K3tog, turn.

*Row 4 (WS):* Yo, purl across to the yo from the previous row. Slip 2 yo's and the first st of the next pair pwise and replace them onto the left needle. P3tog, turn.

Repeat Rows 3 and 4 until all but one pair on each side have been knitted.

**Return to working around** Replace the sts that have been held on waste yarn to their respective needles. There should be 14 sts on each. (If I changed colors for the heel, I drop the heel color now and pick up the main color again.)

*Rnd 1 (RS):* Yo, knit to center back.

*Rnd 2:* On N1, knit across to the last 2 sts. They should be 2 yo's from the preceding row. Sl them kwise, then sl the first st from N2 kwise and return all 3 sts onto N2. On N2, k3tog, then knit across. On N3, knit across to the last st. Sl that st and the first 2 sts on N4 (which should be yo's), return them to N4, and k3tog with N3. Otherwise there will be 13 sts remaining on N3 and 15 on N4. You'll see when you knit it. On N4, knit across. There should now be 14 sts on each needle. Double-check this and adjust if necessary.

**Instep** Knit every rnd until foot measures 2" (5 cm) less than desired overall length from back of heel to tip of toe. (I like to try my socks on as I knit because if they are a little snug, they will need to be a bit longer than my actual instep

length to allow for the sideways stretch.)

**Toe** (If I am going to change colors for the toe, I often knit 2 rounds with the new color before beginning to decrease, so that the decreases will appear in the new color instead of the instep color.)

*Rnd 1:* On N1 and N3, knit across to the last 3 sts, k2tog, k1. On N2 and N4, k1, ssk, knit across.

*Rnd 2:* Knit around.

Repeat these two rnds until there are 4 sts on each needle (16 sts). Place sts from N3 onto N2, and sts from N1 onto N4, so that there are 8 sts on one needle for the top of the toe and 8 sts on another needle for the bottom of the toe. Join the remaining sts with Kitchener stitch.

**Knitting the sock toe up**

**Toe** CO 16 sts, using a provisional cast on. (After finishing the sock, you will join the toe sts with Kitchener stitch.) Divide sts onto four needles, being careful not to twist the row, and join. Knit two rnds, then work inc as follows.

*Rnd 1:* On N1 and N3, knit across to the last 2 sts on the needle, increase 1 st by knitting into the st below the next st, k2. On N2 and N4, k2, inc 1 st by knitting into the st below the st just knitted, knit across.

## WORKING STITCHES

I define working stitches as the number of stitches in the main body of the sock. This number gives me a designing landmark. It usually remains constant from the cuff to the toe, this number tells me how many stitches I should have on the needles when working the leg instep. Knowing the number of working stitches also helps me to see heels, toes, and cuffs as interchangeable design elements and to figure out Fair Isle or mosaic color patterns. It also helps me know whether I've dropped or added a stitch. For more on working stitches, gauge, and related topics, see p. 59. ◈

*Rnd 2:* Knit around.

Repeat these two rnds until there are 14 sts on each needle. (If I want to change color, I knit one more rnd before switching to the instep color.)

**Instep** Knit foot to 2" (5 cm) less than the desired length from tip of toe to back of heel. Knit to the end of N3 and stop. (If I want to work the heel in a different color, I begin with that here. I do not break the main color yarn, but simply drop it and pick it up later.)

**Heel** Work an hourglass heel, the same as for cuff down sock.

**Leg** Knit until leg measures 4" (10 cm) or desired length.

**Cuff** Work k1, p1 ribbing for 1½" (3.8 cm).

**Top edge** Finish with invisible bind off (p. 70).

**Finishing** Finishing techniques are like the foundation of a house. It's what you don't see that matters. Good finishing not only makes a garment neater and stronger, but more comfortable as well. This is especially true of socks.

When you want maximum comfort for sensitive feet, try to knit the entire sock in a continuous yarn, rather than breaking off or tying on new yarns. Variegated yarns put a lot of color into a sock without the necessary yarn changes that other colorwork requires.

Tie on new yarns at a place where the knot or join won't be so readily felt. I like to change colors at the center back on the leg, but I avoid color changes in any high-wear areas.

Work ends in loosely, mimicking the stitch size and stretch of the surrounding sock fabric. If the ends are drawn too tight, that area will not stretch like the rest of the sock. When working gusset heels, I like to secure any ends

photo: Lynne Vogel

▲ Follow the steps in the drawing below to make this gap invisible.

▲ Thread the yarn end through the first loop on the right side of the gap. Then close the gap by inserting the needle into the loop on the left side and pulling the yarn tight. Then go back through the loop on the right and work the yarn tail into the wrong side of the sock.

photo: Lynne Vogel

▲ The miraculously closed gap is now neat and secure.

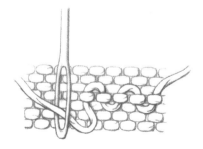

▲ Finish yarn ends by working them loosely into the wrong side of the fabric.

**TIPS**

❖ I keep a file card or small notebook with my knitting so I can write down important numbers such as the number of rounds between the ribbing and the heel. This makes it a lot easier to make a mate. When knitting the mate, I mark every ten rounds in the leg and instep with a small piece of waste yarn so I don't have to count the rounds repeatedly.

❖ When working with four double-pointed needles, I find it is easier to work from a needle if both ends of that needle are resting on top of the needles to either side.

❖ Having a hard time undoing a knot? Insert the tip of a knitting needle or a blunt darning needle into the center of the knot and wiggle. The knot will soon open. ❖

up the inside of the selvedge of the placket, because I feel them less there than if ends are tucked along the bottom or top of the heel. This may seem finicky to some, and may be unnecessary for many, but for those who like their socks to give evenly, end placement is something to think about.

To finish the top of a cuff, I thread the cast-on tail through a blunt needle and use it to connect the cast-on row with a join that's almost invisible. Then I work the rest of the tail down the inside of the closest rib.

**HOW TO FIT YOUR FEET** Proper fit is one of the reasons for making a custom pattern. Consider this when measuring your foot. Do you like a sock to be snug so that it doesn't move around on your foot, or does it feel better when there is enough play so you can wiggle your toes? I find that there is a difference between a snug sock and a tight sock. A snug sock has a small amount of air space which makes it warmer. A tight sock feels too constricted and also releases body heat too fast. Socks that are too tight also tend to wear more quickly. Of course loose socks can really get in the

The basic sock pattern can be broken down into seven parts: the cuff, leg, heel, foot, and toe, plus the cast on and bind off. There are many ways to knit each of these parts and you can easily interchange these elements to create your personal favorite pattern. Also, if you remember how to work the elements you have chosen, all you need is this "shorthand" version of the pattern to remind you what you've done when it's time to work the mate or another pair.

For example, here's a sample of a shorthand pattern of the basic sock pattern.

**Yarn**: 12 wpi

**Gauge:** 6½ spi

**Needle size:** 3

**Direction:** Cuff down

**Cast on:**   K on double, 112 sts, *ssk, p2tog* first rnd.

**Working sts:** 56

**Cuff:** K1, p1 rib, 14 rnds

**Leg:**   St st 45 rnds

**Heel:** Hourglass, 9 dec

**Foot:**   St st 52 rnds

**Toe:** Wedge to 16

**Bind off:** Kitchener

Here's my translation of what these abbreviations mean. Working from the cuff down, I used a stretchy cast on, casting on 112 stitches, then reduced by half to the working number of 56 stitches. I knit 14 rounds in k1, p1 rib, then changed to stockinette stitch and knit 45 rounds before beginning the heel. In working my hourglass heel, I short-rowed 9 times, leaving 9 pairs of decreases before I turned the heel. Then I knit 52 rounds of stockinette stitch in the foot before I started a wedge toe. I worked the decreases in the wedge until I had 16 stitches remaining in the round, then grafted them together with Kitchener stitch. ◈

way. You may want to take into consideration the type of footwear you will be wearing with the sock before you determine the sizing. It's also helpful to measure the circumference of a favorite commercial sock in its "resting" state off the foot and analyze the pattern. Choose a favorite pair that fits the way you like socks to fit.

The photos below show how to take four basic measurements. These are all you really need to knit a nice sock.

photo: Lynne Vogel

▲ Do I have to wear these? They're way too big!

photo: Lynne Vogel

▲ That's better!

photo: Lynne Vogel

To measure your **foot length**, stand on a ruler with your heel and the end of the ruler against a flat wall or door. Make sure the small numbers are next to the wall. (Use a ruler that begins at zero. Some rulers have an extra bit before the zero point.) Put your full weight on the ruler and measure in a straight line to the tip of your longest toe.

photo: Lynne Vogel

Using a tape measure, find the **circumference** at the widest part of the ball of your foot. This is the most important measurement you can make, because the sock should fit best at the ball. This measurement determines the number of stitches in your sock. Usually the sock will stretch enough to accommodate the rest of the foot.

photo: Lynne Vogel

Measure the distance from the **bottom of the heel** to the **top of the desired cuff**. Do this by standing and placing a ruler next to your foot. It is nice to have someone else do this for you for a really accurate measurement. This measurement combines heel, leg, and cuff elements.

photo: Lynne Vogel

Flex your foot and place a ruler at the bend above your instep. This is the **instep line**. Hold the ruler at that line and point your foot to take the measurement from your instep line to the tip of your longest toe, then add ¼ inch (6 mm). Use this measurement for placing an afterthought heel.

**SAMPLING, YARN, AND GAUGE** It is important to establish a desirable weight and density of fabric, but everyone's knitting is unique, and if you're working with handspun, every yarn is unique too. You have to take all this into account when making two important decisions about socks—what size needles to use, and how many working stitches to use. There are some shortcuts you can use to choose a ballpark figure for getting started with a project, but sampling is indispensable if you want to fine-tune your knitting.

Suitable sock fabric is usually a bit denser than fabric for other wearables such as hats and sweaters. When I first started knitting socks, I was uncomfortable with knitting a dense fabric and it took me a few pairs before I could graduate to smaller needles. I still love and wear those early socks that were knitted in my comfort zone. Twisted Sisters will all agree that it is better to enjoy knitting than it is to worry whether it is perfect. Now I try to knit a sock fabric that is dense enough to be durable, but not so dense that it is difficult to knit nor so stiff that it is uncomfortable to wear.

**Make a swatch tube** Because I seem to knit a bit tighter in the round, I end up with a slightly different gauge than when working back and forth with the same yarn and needles. For this reason I knit my sample swatches in the round.

photo: Lynne Vogel

◀ Rachael knitted these socks with the same pattern and same needles. Different yarns make different socks. That's why you need to sample. The sock on the left is from roving shown on p. 6. The sock on the right is knit from stretchy commercial sock yarn.

I used to avoid doing this because I would cast on and start fresh every time I worked a new yarn. Now I keep a running swatch tube going all the time. Since I leave the needles in it, I can pick it up, tie on a new yarn, and just knit, changing needle size whenever I want.

I usually work in stockinette stitch, using the same number of working stitches as my typical socks. This way I can see my color developing in the endless spiral that will appear in the finished piece. If I change needle sizes, I often increase or decrease the stitch number so the tube stays about the same circumference or sock size.

The advantage of making a tube comes when I really love what I see in the swatch. I just drop the knitting that has come before it (p. 61) and proceed, making a sock with the bit I like. By the same token, if I start a sock and don't like it, I turn it into a sample swatch and keep adding different yarns to it as I knit.

◀ A sample swatch tube.

Wonderful creative ideas and unexpected color combinations emerge from this method.

Sampling gives me a chance to find the proper gauge and weight of fabric for my yarn. This is indispensable with handspun because my own yarns don't come with suggested needle size and gauge suggestions. Starting with a tube and then turning the sample swatch into a sock gives me the opportunity to try many yarns and stitches and be able to wear the fruits of the sampling. Just think of all the great socks you would have if you worked all your samples as tubes!

**Counting wraps per inch** Yarns come in many weights or thicknesses. Choosing the proper needle size can be a challenge, especially with handspun yarn. Since there is a relationship between yarn thickness, needle size, and gauge, one shortcut is to measure the yarn and then refer to the gauge chart (p. 58) to select suitable needles.

One method of measuring yarn thickness is to wrap the yarn around a

▶ To count wraps per inch, slowly turn the dowel and roll on the yarn without applying tension.

ruler and count the number of wraps that will fit into 1" (2.5 cm). There is more than one way to do this, and how you determine wraps per inch may be influenced by how you plan to use the yarn. Since I am measuring yarn for knitting, I want to acknowledge the loft of the yarn, since no matter how tightly a yarn is knitted, it will fluff up to some degree once it is off the needles.

To measure wraps per inch and still maintain loft, I like to roll my yarn onto a dowel or other handy cylindrical object,

KNITTING SOCKS

# GAUGE CHART

| Yarn size, in wraps per inch and cm | Gauge Sts per inch, stockinette | Recommended needle size US | Metric | Needle size you use to obtain gauge |
|---|---|---|---|---|
| 22 | 10 | 0 | 2 mm | |
| 18 | 8¾ | 1 | 2.25 mm | |
| 14 | 7½ | 2 | 2.75 mm | |
| 12 | 6½ | 3 | 3.25 mm | |
| 10 | 6 | 4 | 3.5 mm | |
| 9 | 5½ | 5 | 3.75 mm | |
| 8 | 5 | 6 | 4.25 mm | |

▲ Figuring how many working stitches to use

such as a knitting needle. After winding off a good length of yarn as I would for knitting, I hold the dowel in one hand and wrap the yarn around a few times to anchor it, then start rolling the yarn loosely onto the dowel. I spin the dowel in my dominant hand while guiding the yarn on smoothly with my nondominant hand. Once I have wound on a few inches of yarn, I'll grab the yarn on the dowel and turn the dowel one or two turns the opposite way that I wound it. This loosens the yarn, allowing it to fluff up on the dowel reaching its maximum potential loft. I make sure that the wraps are sitting right next to each other without spaces, but I don't scrunch the wraps any closer than they would sit naturally beside one another. I measure the number over several inches to check for inconsistencies in the yarn.

**Using a gauge chart** Most knitters can knit a particular weight of yarn to a certain number of stitches per inch or cm, the variable factor being the size of needles used to obtain that gauge. The chart above suggests a gauge in stitches per inch (cm) for a range of yarn weights that are suitable for socks. If your knitting is not unusually tight or loose, the chart will give you an idea of what needle size to use to obtain the stated gauge for each yarn.

If your needles tend to slip out of your stitches, use smaller needles. If your stitches are so tight that it is difficult to slide them along the needle, use a size larger than recommended.

After you determine what needle size you need to obtain a certain gauge, write it into the chart for quick future reference.

**Figuring how many working stitches to use** The chart on page 59 will help you decide how many working stitches you need to make socks of different sizes and when working at different gauges. The numbers on the left side are circumferences for feet from a baby's 4-inch (10 cm) foot to a large adult's 10 ½-inch (26.5 cm) foot. The numbers across the top are for gauge, in stitches per inch/cm over stockinette stitch.

Determine your gauge and read down that column to the desired circumference to find the number of working stitches you need.

All numbers have been rounded to the nearest even number in a regular sequence, meaning that they are all multiples of two. If you need a multiple of four and you don't find it on the chart, add or subtract two to get the next multiple of four. Two stitches one way or the other should not make a critical difference to a stretchy sock. If knitting an inelastic stitch, such as Fair Isle or mosaic, always round up to the higher number.

**THE SOCK AS A TUBE** A sock is a tube with embellishments. The simplest stocking is a leg warmer—a tube with ribbing at both ends and maybe a taper

| Circumference | | Stitches per inch | | | | | | | | | | | | |
|---|---|---|---|---|---|---|---|---|---|---|---|---|---|---|
| inches | (cm) | 4.5 | 5 | 5.5 | 6 | 6.5 | 7 | 7.5 | 8 | 8.5 | 9 | 9.5 | 10 | 10.5 |
| 10.5 | (26.5) | 48 | 52 | 58 | 64 | 68 | 72 | 76 | 84 | 88 | 94 | 100 | 106 | 110 |
| 10 | (25.5) | 44 | 50 | 56 | 60 | 64 | 70 | 74 | 80 | 84 | 90 | 94 | 100 | 104 |
| 9.5 | (24) | 42 | 48 | 52 | 58 | 62 | 66 | 72 | 76 | 80 | 84 | 90 | 94 | 100 |
| 9 | (23) | 40 | 44 | 48 | 54 | 58 | 62 | 68 | 72 | 76 | 82 | 86 | 90 | 94 |
| 8.5 | (21.5) | 38 | 42 | 46 | 50 | 56 | 60 | 64 | 68 | 72 | 76 | 81 | 86 | 90 |
| 8 | (20.5) | 36 | 40 | 44 | 48 | 53 | 56 | 60 | 64 | 68 | 72 | 76 | 80 | 84 |
| 7.5 | (19) | 34 | 38 | 42 | 46 | 48 | 52 | 56 | 60 | 64 | 68 | 70 | 74 | 78 |
| 7 | (18) | 32 | 36 | 38 | 42 | 46 | 48 | 52 | 56 | 58 | 62 | 66 | 68 | 72 |
| 6.5 | (16.5) | 30 | 32 | 34 | 38 | 42 | 44 | 48 | 52 | 56 | 58 | 62 | 64 | 68 |
| 6 | (15) | 26 | 30 | 32 | 36 | 38 | 42 | 44 | 48 | 50 | 54 | 56 | 60 | 62 |
| 5.5 | (14) | 24 | 28 | 30 | 32 | 34 | 38 | 42 | 44 | 46 | 48 | 52 | 54 | 58 |
| 5 | (12.5) | 22 | 26 | 28 | 30 | 32 | 34 | 38 | 40 | 42 | 44 | 48 | 50 | 52 |
| 4.5 | (11.5) | 20 | 22 | 24 | 28 | 30 | 32 | 34 | 36 | 38 | 40 | 42 | 44 | 48 |
| 4 | (10) | 18 | 20 | 22 | 24 | 26 | 28 | 30 | 32 | 34 | 36 | 38 | 40 | 42 |

▲ Circumference at ball of foot is measured in inches and centimeters. Stitches per inch is the gauge for stockinette stitch.

along the way. Then comes the tube sock—a tube with one open end and one closed end. The addition of a turned heel enhances the fit and comfort and turns the tube into the modern sock with which we are all familiar.

When I consider the body of the sock as a tube and the heels, toes, and cuffs as additions, I can juggle the different parts of the whole and remove or reassemble them in any order, and I am not stuck working from one end to the other. I can start anywhere and go in any direction. This frees me to use my ideas and materials any way I choose.

**Knit stitch anatomy** The knitted row is really a squiggly line, as you have probably noticed when you have had to unravel your work. In a fabric, each row is linked to its neighbors and becomes a strong elastic three-dimensional mesh. But one row linked to nothing looks like this:

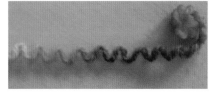

photo: Lynne Vogel

If you turn this upside down, it looks the same as before. It becomes apparent from this that there are now two possible rows and therefore two directions to knit from each row: one going up and one down.

Socks don't have to MATCH exactly. As long as they *coordinate* in an obvious way they will look like a pair.
—TWISTED SISTERS' TIP

These rows are staggered by one-half stitch. Knit stockinette stitch, and this stagger is invisible. Knitting in the round makes a virtually seamless fabric starting at any point in the sock. But if you add a pattern, such as Fair Isle, the stagger appears. This can be a design element if repeated at intervals in the sock. Otherwise it could look like a mistake.

This wonderful little squiggle is also a diagram for Kitchener stitch (p. 71). When you join two rows of knitting to make a seamless fabric, you are making this squiggly line. Kitchener stitch is very

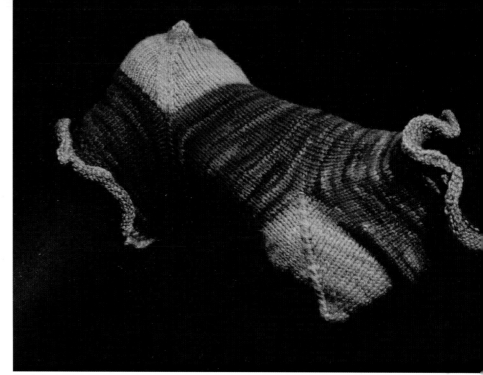

photo: Jim Ann Howard

▲ The Push-Me/Pull-You sock. This whimsical piece started as a sample tube.

▲ Row B is the row or round to be removed. When you pick up the stitches of row A onto one needle and the stitches of row C onto another needle, the stitches will be staggered or offset from each other. When you dismantle a tube and remove an entire round of stitches, you will pick up the same number of stitches on round A and round C. But when you remove a partial round to knit an afterthought heel, you will pick up an even number of stitches on one round and an odd number on the other round.

simply the reverse of removing a row of knitting.

**Design opportunities** Now I'm knitting gaily along on a little tube of stockinette stitch. What next? Since I can knit in either direction, I have the option of deciding just where I want to place this particular piece of knitting within the sock. If I want to complete the whole sock in the yarn I'm working with, I will knit from the top down, finish the sock at the toe, and then come back, pick up the stitches in the other direction and knit a cuff, often choosing k1, p1 rib so I can finish the cuff with invisible bind off.

Sometimes I have a tiny ball of yarn, a precious piece I've saved for just the right moment. I can knit the ball into a tube to see just how far it will go, then divide the tube in half to use in a pair of socks. This way I can utilize every inch of my precious yarn. I might prefer to display this piece on the foot near the toe end rather than up near the cuff. Either way, I can decide exactly where I want it to go, then knit the rest of the sock in a different yarn or combination of yarns.

**Dismantling a tube** In order to use a particular piece of a tube, it must be removed from the unwanted knitting that surrounds it. This same technique comes in handy for removing and replacing worn-out heels and toes. To dismantle a tube you will need four circular needles (CNs) the same size or smaller than used for knitting the tube.

1. Dismantling the tube requires that you remove one rnd of knitting. Decide what rnd this will be. It will be adjacent to (directly above or below) the portion of knitting you want to save. Mark the first st in the rnd that is to be removed.

2. You will place all the sts from the rnds above and below the marked rnd onto four CNs. Start with the first st of the rnd below it. Insert the CN into this st, then pick up half of the sts in the rnd. Center the sts on this needle and use it as a st holder.

   Take another CN and pick up the remaining sts of the rnd. Don't try to put all the sts in one rnd on one CN, as that stretches the sts at the ends. Using two needles keeps the work flat and easy to handle.

3. With another CN, begin to pick up sts from the rnd above the marked rnd that you will remove. Proceed as before, putting all the sts of the rnd onto two CNs. There should be the same number of sts on each needle.

4. Clip the center st of the rnd to be removed. With a BN or knitting needle, unravel the row st by st. This gives you a chance to be sure you put the correct sts on the holder when picking up the rnds.

To remove a row of knitting, the stitches of the rows on either side of it must be put onto a holding device. If you don't have circular needles, use a BN and thread them onto waste yarn until ready to knit.

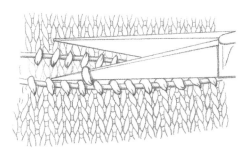

▲ When all stitches of both rounds are on the circular needles, clip the center stitch of the row to be removed.

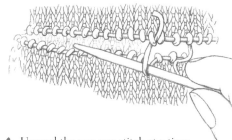

▲ Unravel the row one stitch at a time.

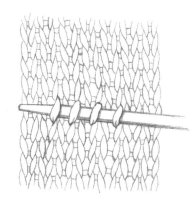

▲ Pick up stitches like this to avoid stitches falling off the needle once the unwanted row is removed.

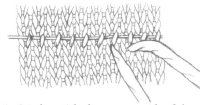

▲ Stitches picked up on one side of the round to be removed.

**SOME OTHER WAYS TO KNIT A SOCK** Most of my own knitting style emerges from using methods I enjoy and avoiding ones I dislike. I used to really dislike working on double-pointed needles and would design an entire piece around avoiding the pointy devils. I've learned a lot from this because I invariably have to go to a lot of trouble to use only the methods I like, and sometimes, as Elizabeth Zimmermann was so fond of saying, even "rediscover" others.

The following two methods can be worked for the most part in the "flat," that is, on a pair of standard knitting needles. The first method makes a seamless tube by working back and forth in a slip stitch pattern. The second method is for knitting a sock as a flat pattern piece, then joining the selvedges with a decorative

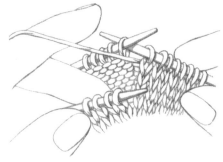

▲ Knitting from two needles onto one. First, knit the stitch on the front needle, then slip the stitch from the back needle.

looking, totally comfortable, and "unfeelable" seam.

**Knitting a tube in the "flat"** This tube is knitted on two needles with a simple slip stitch pattern and is open at both ends when completed. You still have to knit your heels, toes, and cuffs with double-pointed needles, but you can complete a lot of the sock this way.

For this technique, you need a pair of knitting needles and one more needle (of any type) the same size, along with two blunt tapestry needles (BNs).

**Starting and knitting a tube**

Cast on an even number of sts in either loop or invisible cast on.

Knit half of the sts, then fold the work in half with the purl sides facing in. Hold the two needles together with the needle points facing right (if you are right handed). Make sure your sts aren't twisted on either of the needles. The needle with the knit sts is N2 and is in back. The needle with cast-on sts is N1 and is in front.

*Row 1:* With a third needle (N3), *wyib, k1 from N1; wyif (between needles) sl 1 from N2*; rep between *'s to

end of row. All sts are now on one needle.

*All subsequent rows:* *Wyb, k1, wyf sl 1* across row.

Always snug the first st so that you don't leave a line of loose sts up the sides of the tube. Continue in this fashion until you reach desired length for leg and foot (cuff, toe, and heel will be added later). As you knit, you will be able to see the tube opening and slide a hand inside.

**Adding a toe** When it's time to make a toe for the sock, try one of these options.

1. Using two BNs and two lengths of waste yarn, slip the sts onto the waste yarn by alternately slipping all even sts onto one BN and all odd sts onto the other BN. Then open the tube and divide the sts from the waste yarn evenly to dp needles.

2. (For the dexterous) Using four dp needles, alternately slip the first half of the odd sts onto one dp, and the first half of the even sts onto another dp, then slip the remaining odds onto a third dp and the remaining evens onto a fourth dp.

Proceed as usual for knitting the toe of your choice.

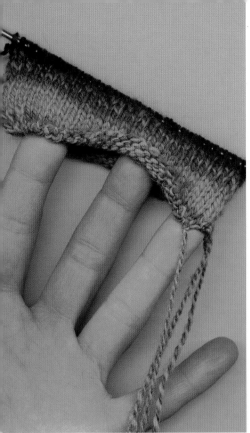

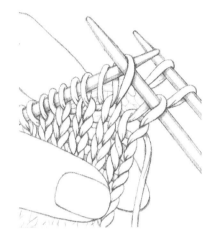

◀ You can see the tube opening as you knit.

photo: Lynne Vogel

▲ Returning stitches from one needle to two needles. The needles on the right are alternately slipping stitches. The needle in front is slipping the knit stitches. The needle in back is slipping the purl stitches.

**Working the cuff** There are several options for making a cuff.

You can make a k1, p1 ribbed cuff simply by substituting p sts for k sts as you begin knitting the flat tube. Follow the directions above for casting on and joining. Then work the ribbing like this: * wyb k1, wyf sl 1, wyf p1, wyf sl 1* across row. Continue for the desired cuff length, then change to * wyb k1, wyf sl1* to make stockinette st.

Or, start your ribbing for your cuff on dp needles. When it comes time to work in stockinette, transfer your sts to straight needles as above and continue in the "flat."

Another approach is to begin with a provisional cast on, make your tube, and then add the cuff last and finish with an invisible bind off.

**Adding the heel** Add an afterthought heel to the sock (see p. 76).

**Knitting a sock back and forth** Socks are usually worked in the round to avoid a cumbersome and uncomfortable seam.

But if you prefer to work back and forth or want to include intarsia patterns in your socks, it is possible to work a flat seam that is so comfortable that it is virtually unnoticeable. Here is how to work a flat sock with a seam up the center back.

This sock is worked flat in k1, p1 ribbing throughout, except for the heel and toe which are worked in the round on dp needles in stockinette stitch. The sock shown here was knitted from various worsted-weight yarns. The springiness of the ribbing accommodates the slightly different weights and they appear as textural differences.

**Yarn:** Worsted-weight, about 10 wpi.

**Gauge:** 24 sts = 4" (10 cm) in k1, p1 rib.

**Needles:** One pair size 6 or 7 (4 mm or 4.5 mm). Five dp needles, two sizes smaller than straight needles, for heels and toes. Blunt darning needle for finishing.

**Cuff and leg** CO 51 sts on straight needles.

*Row 1 (RS):* Sl1 kwise, *k1, p1* across row, k2.

*Row 2 (WS):* Sl1 pwise, *p1, k1* across row, p2.

Continue in pattern for desired length to instep line (see p. 55).

## Mark heel opening

*Row 1 (RS):* K13. Place these sts on a foot-long piece of waste yarn. K25. Place the last 13 sts of the row onto another piece of waste yarn, then CO 13 sts in invisible cast on, using waste yarn as the removable strand. *Row 2 (WS):* Sl1 pwise, *p1, k1* across row. CO 13 sts with invisible cast on, using waste yarn from previous row as the removable strand.

**Foot** Continue in pattern to desired length, 2" (5 cm) from end of toe.

**Toe** With dp needles two sizes smaller, knit the row, dividing the sts on the needles as follows: 12, 13, 13, 13. Join and knit one round. Work decs to make a round toe.

**Seam** To finish the seam, you may work the following flat seam for the foot and leg seams, or you may choose to work the flat seam on the foot of the sock only and work your choice of an invisible seam on the leg.

To make a flat seam, thread a BN with a few yards of yarn. With RS facing you, work a duplicate st over the selvedge st on one side of the seam, then another duplicate st over the corresponding selvedge st on the other side of the seam. When you return to the first side, insert the needle through the back of the loop of the previous selvedge stitch of that side, then work a duplicate stitch, reinserting the needle into the front of the loop of the stitch below. Work the corresponding selvedge stitch on the other side of the seam in the same way and so on until you have finished the seam. Pull your yarn only tight enough

photo: Lynne Vogel

◀ This is how a flat sock looks before you seam it. The stitches for the heel are on waste yarn.

photo: Lynne Vogel

▶ Linda knitted this sock back and forth on two needles, then seamed it and added the heel.

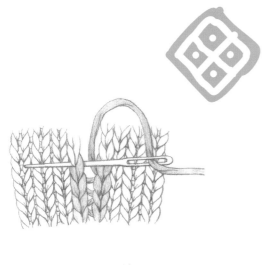

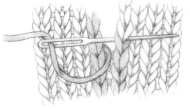

▲ Work duplicate stitch into each of the selvedge stitches on each side of the seam. Keep tension loose so the seam doesn't draw up.

to mimic the stitch beneath so that your seam will not draw up.

**Heel** When you have completed the seams, put the sts from the heel opening onto four dp needles two sizes smaller, and work your choice of afterthought

heels. The heel on the sock shown here is the double center decrease afterthought heel.

photo: Lynne Vogel

**METHODS OF CASTING ON** Socks require an elastic cast on. All too often a tight cast on makes an otherwise good pair of socks hard to put on or uncomfortable to wear. The following cast ons are chosen especially for their ability to stretch.

### Provisional, or invisible, cast on

Provisional or invisible cast on is the bare bones of design knitting. Use this cast on

◀ After seaming, slip the stitches from the waste yarn onto double-pointed needles to begin the afterthought heel.

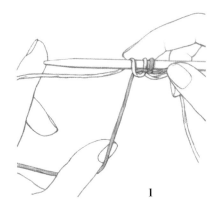

1

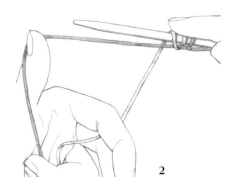

2

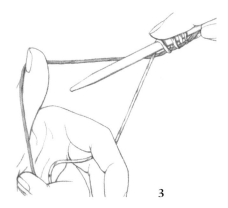

3

◀ The provisional cast on. 1: Wrap the working yarn (light color), 2: Anchor with waste yarn (dark color), 3: wrap again with the working yarn.

and you'll be able to knit in both directions from the starting row. This cast on also stands alone as an elastic edge for k1, p1 rib. Just substitute your main yarn for the waste yarn.

1. Tie a slipknot near the end of your working yarn, slip the loop onto your needle, and tighten it down.

2. Use a piece of waste yarn as long as the row you wish to cast on plus 12" (30.5 cm) and tie a slipknot near one end of it. With the needle in your right hand and the point facing left, slide the loop of the waste yarn onto the needle and snug it next to the first loop. Hold the tails of both yarns in your right hand to keep them out of the way.

3. Insert your left index finger between the working yarn (A) and the waste yarn (B) from behind and twist your finger 90 degrees counterclockwise. Slide your left thumb between A and B next to your index finger and spread the two yarns apart. Now your index finger is holding A and your thumb is holding B. Hold the yarns under ten-sion by grabbing both tails in your third, fourth, and little fingers. Twist the yarns 90 degrees counterclockwise and wrap A around needle (1).

4. *Twist clockwise 180 degrees (2) and wrap A around the needle (3). Twist counterclockwise 180 degrees and wrap A*. Repeat * to * until you have the desired number of sts. (Never wrap B around the needles.)

5. When you begin to knit, make sure the waste yarn is caught under the first st to anchor the loop.

6. Leave waste yarn in place until you are ready to use the sts it is holding. When you are ready to use those sts, insert needles into them, dividing them equally on the needles, then remove the waste yarn.

**Loop, or simple, cast on** Most of us learned to knit with this cast on. Simple as it is, it is a versatile option that is the basis for my stretchy cast on. It is also indispensable for knitting piggy toes and gloves.

1. Tie a slipknot near the end of your working yarn. Slip the loop onto your needle and tighten it down.

2. *With the needle facing left in your right hand, lay the yarn against the front of your left thumb which is at

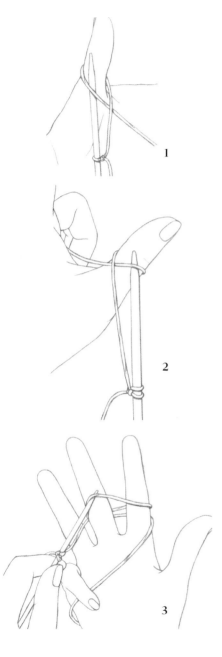

◀ The simple, or loop, cast on. 1: The knit loop. 2: The purl loop. 3: Holly Jean's method.

three o'clock. Turn your thumb to twelve o'clock and take it behind the needle pulling the yarn with it. Slide your needle under the loop of yarn on the front of your thumb from left to right. Slip the loop along the needle and cinch it down*. Repeat * to * until you have the desired number of sts (1).

For the finicky: The directions above are for making a knit stitch. If you want to cast on a purl stitch, twist the loop in the opposite direction by holding your thumb at three o'clock in front of the working yarn. Take your thumb and the yarn away from you and bring your thumb to twelve o'clock. Then bring your thumb in front of the needle and take it to three o'clock making a loop around your thumb. Slide your needle under the loop on the front of your thumb from right to left, transfer the loop to your needle, and cinch it down (2).

Would you rather hold the yarn in your right hand? Try the method my twelve-year-old niece, Holly Jean, made up. Make a peace sign with your right forefinger and middle finger, wrap the yarn counterclockwise all the way around both fingers, then slip the loop onto the needle and tighten down (3).

photo: Lynne Vogel

photo: Lynne Vogel

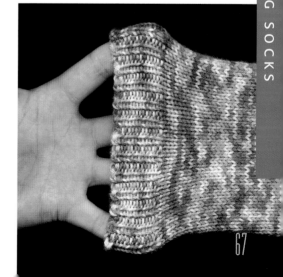

▶ The stretchy cast on, relaxed and stretched.

**Stretchy cast on (for k1, p1 rib)** This two-row cast on is marvelously stretchy and springs right back into shape. No more tight cuffs!

1. *Row 1:* With simple cast on, make double the number of sts that you need. Adjust if needed to make a multiple of 4 sts.
2. *Row 2:* *K2tog, p2tog* across the row. To cast on in the round, work row two, then evenly distribute the remaining stitches on four needles and join the round.

**Ruffled cast on** This makes a wavy ruffled edge at the top of a sock and looks amazing in energized singles yarns.

1. With simple cast on, make double the number of desired sts. Join rnd.
2. Knit 4 to 6 rows or rnds in stockinette.
3. K2tog for one rnd.
4. Begin your favorite rib.

**Long tail cast on** This flexible cast on is a favorite of many. It isn't very flexible, though, if it is done too tightly. One way to make sure you aren't pulling the yarn too tight is to stretch your stitches out on the needle as you go along. If they don't stretch on the needle, they won't stretch when you wear them either. Make sure you can still recognize the loft in the yarn as you work. It should look fluffy like it does in a skein and be easy to knit off the needle. You can cast on to a needle several sizes larger than the needles you will be working with, but even then, if you pull the yarn beyond its normal appearance, the stitches will still be too tight. Keep a loose hand and you will be satisfied with the results.

▼ Debby knit her ruffle in garter st with energized single yarn.

1. Wind off a length of working yarn that is four times longer than your desired row. Tie a slipknot and cinch the loop

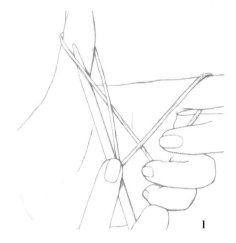

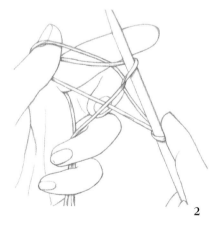

▲ The long tail cast on. 1: Slip needle under loop on thumb. 2: Wrap working yarn around needle and pull through thumb loop.

down on your needle, letting the long tail hang down.

2. Pinch your index finger and thumb together and insert them between the working yarn (A) and the tail (B), making sure that B hangs over your thumb and A hangs over your index finger. Grab both yarns with your remaining fingers and hold the yarns under tension.

3. *Rotate the yarns 90 degrees clockwise. Slide your needle under the loop that is formed on your left thumb (1). Reach back to grab A with your needle, and pull it through the loop formed by B (2). Cinch B down making sure only A wraps around the needle*. Repeat * to * until you have the desired number of sts.

**Picot cast on** This cast on leaves a decorative bumpy edge on a k1, p1 rib. Combined with a twisted rib, it looks very refined indeed.

1. Wind off a length of working yarn that is four times longer than your desired row. At that point, loop the yarn as in simple cast on and slip the loop onto the needle. You should now be holding the yarn just like you would for long tail cast on with B (the tail) in

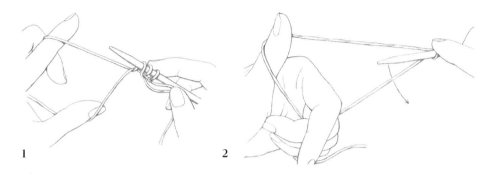

▲ The picot cast on. 1: Work one long tail cast on, rotate hand, and wrap yarn. 2: Rotate hand back to secure the stitch.

front and A (the working yarn) in back.

2. *Cast on 1 st as for long tail cast on, tighten that st, then rotate your left hand 90 degrees clockwise, wrap your needle back under A (1), and rotate 90 degrees counterclockwise* (2). Repeat * to * until you have the desired number of sts, ending with a long tail cast on.

**METHODS OF BINDING OFF** Comfort is important. There are lots of ways to bind off but many leave an inelastic hard edge. Those included here have enough stretch to make them comfortable. Kitchener stitch is included as a bind off since it is used to finish toes and afterthought heels.

**Simple bind off** Use this to close the end of a tube or a round toe.

1. Break the yarn and thread it through a blunt needle.

2. Run the yarn through the remaining loops on the needles and cinch tight. I like to run the yarn through twice for strength.

▲ The simple bind off.

**Invisible bind off for k1, p1 rib** Well worth the extra time, this bind off makes a beautiful rounded edge in 1 × 1 rib that not only looks flawlessly finished, but is very stretchy as well and springs back to shape every time. It is worked with a blunt needle (BN), like Kitchener stitch. These directions are for working in the round.

Measure off enough yarn to go around the sock four times, plus a few inches. Break the end and thread the tail through BN. Hold your work to be bound off in your left hand and the BN in your right hand.

1. Begin casting off with a knit st (K). Run the BN through the K from back to front and then through the purl (P) from front to back. Pull the yarn all the

way through both sts and gently snug the yarn. Slip both sts from the needle, or allow them to slide to the needle tip until the next step is completed.

2. *Take the BN back to the first K, run the BN through from front to back, and slip this st off the needle, if you've not previously done so. Pass BN in

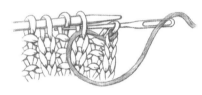

front of the P st to the next K st and run the BN through the K st from back to front. Pull the yarn all the way through and gently snug.

3. Return to the previous P st and insert

BN through it from back to front, slip P st from needle. Pull yarn through

and snug. Passing BN behind the K st, insert the BN through the next P st from front to back. Return to previous K st*.

4. Repeat between *'s until last P in round is bound off. Insert the BN into the previous K from front to back and then through the very first K of the round from back to front. Snug, then insert the BN into the previous P from back to front, then through the very first P of the round from front to back. Bury yarn tail into rib by inserting BN through P from front to back and finish the tail by camouflaging it into the rib.

**Single crochet bind off** This bind off is moderately stretchy and very useful for casting off from a decorative pattern,

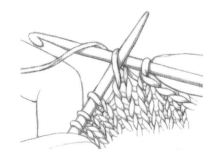

▲ Pull yarn through next stitch.

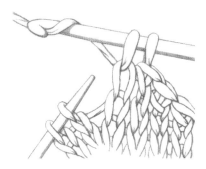

▲ Pull yarn through both loops on hook; one loop will remain.

such as shell stitch. You'll need a crochet hook with diameter similar to the knitting needle size you have been using.

1. Insert the crochet hook into the first st kwise, wrap the yarn around the hook, and pull a loop though the st (chain one). Cinch the yarn down on the hook.

2. *Insert the hook into the next st kwise and chain one. There will be two loops on your hook. Wrap the yarn around the hook and pull a loop through both those loops*. Repeat * to * until you have no more sts. Break yarn, pull end through last loop, and tighten.

**Rolled cuff bind off** This makes a decorative edging on a cuff. It slants and rolls back on itself. Use energized singles yarn.

1. At the top of the leg, knit 4 to 6 rnds in stockinette st with an energized singles yarn.

2. Bind off with single crochet bind off.

**Kitchener stitch, or grafting** So often I hear the complaint, "Oh, I hate Kitchener stitch." This saddens me

because it is one of the most useful techniques in knitting. When I was about eighteen, I took knitting instruction from a woman who ran a knitting design shop. She had designed a number of lovely pieces and she would help you through the knitting process if you bought the yarn from her and worked her design. I chose a lovely emerald green mohair to knit as a V-neck cardigan for my mom because of the continuous cable that ran along the hem, curved around the front opening to become the front edging, and met in the back of the neck. It was elegant and smart looking and I knew Mom would love it.

The entire time I was knitting this, I was wondering how I could make the cable come together at the back of the neck and look seamless. When I finally got there, the designer took it from me and told me she was going to complete the cable herself because it was "her secret" and she didn't want anyone stealing her designs. If I didn't know how to do the magic, I couldn't steal it. This heightened my curiosity far more than if she had shown me how to finish things myself. Her little secret was Kitchener stitch.

photo: Lynne Vogel

◀ The rolled cuff bind off.

I learned how to put things together by taking them apart, and Kitchener is no exception. I finally understood the stitch by removing a row one stitch at a time and following the tail with a blunt needle full of yarn to make a new row. I couldn't get Kitchener straight until I did this. Now I can graft pieces of fabric together in my sleep, knitwise or purlwise.

Working Kitchener on socks, the stitches to be worked are usually held on two needles and pulled off the needles one by one as they are worked into the stitch. I have worked it many times on larger garments by laying the two pieces to be joined flat on a table so that I can see the way my stitches line up. It is easier to understand the stitch this way, but impractical for socks. I have developed a rhythm to help me remember the process. Let's use a wedge toe as an example.

1. Make sure that half of the sts in the round are on one needle, N1, and the other half are on another needle, N2. Hold N1 in front and N2 in back, with the last worked st at the right end of N2.

2. Measure off a length of yarn and thread it into a blunt needle (BN). I determine this length by measuring the width of the area to be closed, multiplying that by four, and adding a few inches for good measure.

3. Run the BN back to front through the first st on N1, and remove the st from N1. Pull the yarn snug.

4. Run the BN front to back through the first st on N2, and remove that st also. Before snugging the yarn all the way, pull up on the strand that emerges from the last stitch from N1. This will open the stitch enough to make it easier to see where to put BN next.

5. Insert the BN front to back into the st you just pulled off N1, then back to front through the next st that is still on N1. Pull this st off N1.

6. Insert the BN back to front into the first st you pulled off N2, then front to back through the next st that is still on N2. Pull this st off N2.

7. Proceed along the row, repeating steps 5 and 6. You'll be inserting the BN front to back, back to front; back to front, front to back, through pairs of sts on N2 and N1, alternately.

8. When you have pulled the last 2 sts off N2 and N1, the yarn will emerge from the last st on N2. Insert it once

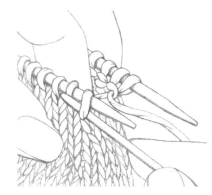

▲ To begin, pull one stitch off N1.

▲ Pull one stitch off N2.

▲ When working stitches from N1, insert the blunt tapestry needle into the first stitch front to back and the next stitch back to front.

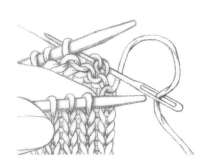

△ When working stitches from N2, insert the blunt tapestry needle into the first stitch back to front and the next stitch front to back.

again, front to back, into the last st of N1. Pull the yarn tail through and secure it in the work.

**RIBBING AND CUFFS** Here are some standard and not-so-standard ribbings for cuffs. The first three look great and perform well whether worked short or long.

The last two look best long, in my opinion. For great texture with optional design possibilities, try the interrupted rib. I get bored working long ribbed cuffs and interrupted rib seems to go faster for me because I can see change along the way. The fancy rib is deeply grooved and very elastic. Couple it with a stretchy cast on and a fancy tulip edge and your socks will never bind at the calves again!

**K2, p2 ribbing** This is the standard stretchy ribbing for socks.

CO a multiple of 4 sts. Divide sts evenly on four needles. Join rnd. K2, p2 until you reach desired length.

When knitting a long ribbed cuff (6–7" [15–18 cm] or more), include a dec rnd when you change from ribbing to stockinette st. This will help the sock fit the ankle better. Dec 4 sts evenly spaced all around. If your gauge is very fine (smaller than 12 sts per inch [2.5 cm]), dec by 8 sts all around (k2tog twice each needle).

**K1, p1 ribbing** Life without the basics is unthinkable. When knitting toe up, work this rib and finish with invisible bind off.

CO a multiple of 2 sts. Divide sts evenly on four needles. Join rnd. K1, p1 until you reach desired length.

**Twisted k1, p1 ribbing** All twisted sisters should know how to do a twisted rib! This rib takes a little more time than an ordinary k1, p1 ribbing, but it is really worth it, both in decorative value and in wearability. This rib draws in more snugly than a regular k1, p1 but it stretches out equally far. CO a multiple

of 2 sts. Use picot cast on for a decorative edge. Divide sts evenly on four needles. Join rnd.

K1 through the back loop (tbl), p1 tbl, twisting every st on every round as you go.

**Fancy ribbing with "tulip" edge** This rib is very cushy, deeply three-dimensional, and stretchy. There is absolutely no binding at the calf with this cuff!

CO twice the desired number of sts, rounding off to a multiple of 5 sts. Use loop cast on. Divide sts evenly on four needles. Join rnd.

*Rnd 1:* *(K2tog) 3 times, (p2tog) twice* all around.

*Rnd 2 and all even rnds:* *K3, p2* all around.

*Rnd 3 and all subsequent odd rnds:* *K1, k1b, k1, p2* all around. K1b means to knit one st in the row below. To do this, insert your needle into the st from the previous row and knit it, then pull off that st with the st on the needle. (Don't make a lifted increase by mistake.)

When worked with this cast on, this ribbing will roll open like the petals of a tulip. To make a straight cuff, use long tail cast on instead.

**Interrupted ribbing** This rib seems to go faster than ribbing all the way down. It is very comfortable, looks nice, and doesn't sag. It isn't quite as stiff as solid ribbing, but stands up well nevertheless.

1. CO a multiple of 4 sts. Divide sts evenly on four needles. Join rnd.

2. Work 8 rnds of *k2, p2* ribbing.

3. Work dec rnd: Knit every st. Work two k2tog, evenly spaced, on each needle (a total of 8 decs in the rnd). I like to knit two p sts together because the dec doesn't show as much. Remember where you made the decs because you will increase at the same positions later. I usually place decs at the first and last pairs of p sts on each needle.

4. Knit 5 more rnds in stockinette. (Note: If your gauge is very fine, you may work more rnds in both sections of the pattern.)

5. Work inc rnd: *K2, p2*. Inc by 2 sts on each needle (8 sts increased in the rnd). To inc, p1 directly above the 2 p sts you knitted together in the dec rnd, then pick up the back of the loop of the st below the st you just purled and p it separately. This is much easier than it sounds.

6. Work 7 more rnds of *k2, p2* ribbing.

Repeat this pattern for the desired length of leg, stopping about 1½" (3.8 cm) above the beginning of the heel. End with k2, p2 ribbing followed by the dec rnd. Knit 12 to 16 rnds in stockinette before beginning heel.

*Note:* If you want to add a simple Fair Isle pattern in the stockinette section (like I did in the sock on p. 25), don't work a dec rnd when changing from ribbing to stockinette. The natural

◀ The ribs. Top to bottom: K1, p1 worked toe up and finished with invisible bind off; twisted k1, p1 with picot cast on; k2, p2 rib; fancy rib with "tulip" edge; interrupted rib.

draw-in of Fair Isle knitting will do that for you.

**HEELS: THE TURNING POINT**
Shaping heels is part of the fun of knitting socks. I'll start with directions for knit-as-you-go heels that you work as you're making a sock. In the next section I'll cover afterthought heels, which you insert into a finished tube.

Both of the following knit-as-you-go heels have merit. One is not better than the other, but you may prefer their different qualities for several reasons. The gusset heel is the standard hand-knit heel. It has several advantages. It can be adapted to fit any size and shape of heel from the short and shallow to the tall and narrow. The placket can be a tiny canvas for colorwork or stitch patterns. It is easy to understand its workings and fun to knit. The only disadvantage is the relative difficulty in replacing it when it is worn through.

The hourglass heel is familiar to us all as the one we see on commercial socks. It is versatile because you can knit it from either direction, toe up or cuff down, with no changes necessary. For directions, see the basic sock pattern on p. 50. It looks great in contrasting yarns, is fun to knit, and is very comfortable to wear. When worn, you can replace it by removing it and knitting an afterthought hourglass heel.

**Knitting a gusset heel** This heel has a straight-sided placket that is worked back and forth. This area is a tiny canvas for interesting stitches. Knit some of the following heel placket suggestions or make up your own.

**Setup** This heel should be worked from the cuff down. When you have reached the desired place for the heel, knit across N1, N2, and N3, then stop. Place the sts from N2 and N3 on waste yarn or just leave them on the needles. You will be working with the sts from N1 and N4 only.

**Knit placket** Knit all the sts from N4 and N1 onto one needle. Purl back. Slipping the first st of every row, work back and forth in stockinette or pattern for desired length. This length should equal the distance from the lowest point on the anklebone to the floor.
Here are two placket variations:
◈ Heel stitch. This is a strong stitch for reinforcing the back of the heel. Knit

photo: Lynne Vogel

across. Purl back. Then repeat the following two rows until placket is desired length.
*Row 1 (RS):* K1; *sl1 wyb, k1*; repeat * to *.
*Row 2 (WS):* Purl back. (Or to make the fabric even tougher, knit back.)
◈ Fair Isle. Work a favorite Fair Isle stitch on the placket to reinforce the fabric and add pizzazz. *K1 in color A, k1 in color B* makes a nice vertically striped fabric. To graph your own pattern, mark the number of sts in your placket onto graph paper and draw pictures or letters onto the squares. Remember to leave one selvedge st on each side of the graph. Follow as for any graph.

**Turn heel** To "turn" the heel, you make a series of short rows. A short row means working partway across the needle, then turning and going back.
*TIP:* It isn't necessary to wrap stitches

in heel turn short rows. The decreases fill in the hole that normally forms at the turn point. Work as follows:
*Row 1 (RS):* Count your sts. K half of them, then k2, ssk, k1, turn.
*Row 2 (WS):* Sl 1, p5, p2tog, p1, turn.
*Row 3 (RS):* Sl 1, Knit to the stitch before the previous decrease, ssk (using the st before the previous dec and the first st after) k1, turn.
*Row 4 (WS):* Sl 1, purl to the stitch before the previous decrease, p2tog, p1, turn.
Repeat Rows 3 and 4, working to the stitch before the dec on each row until all sts have been worked. End with a WS row.

**Shape gussets** Return sts from N2 and N3 to needles if you removed them before beginning the heel. Knit to center back, then place sts on three needles as follows. On N1, knit from center back to edge of the heel, pick up one st for each selvedge loop along the side of the placket, and k the first st of the next needle. On N2, knit across the instep, stopping before the last st. On N3, knit that last st, pick up one st for each selvedge loop along the side of the placket, and k the remaining sts of the heel.

*Rnd 1:* Knit.

*Rnd 2:* On N1, knit across to the last two sts, k2tog. On N2, k. On N3, ssk the first two sts, k across.

Repeat these two rnds until you have decreased to your original working number of sts. In other words, if you had 56 sts when you started knitting the heel, you should decrease the gussets until 56 sts remain.

At this point, before knitting the foot, divide sts evenly onto four needles. I sometimes like to knit the entire gusset on four needles. It depends on my gauge. For a fine gauge, I find it easier to work with four needles instead of three. If I'm working a stitch pattern, it's often easier to keep track of incs and decs if I divide sts with respect to the repeats, so I use three or four needles, whichever works better.

**Replacing worn gusset heels** Gusset heels often wear out at the very bottom of the heel in the part that is included in the gusset area. To mend this really well, it is best to reknit the entire heel and gusset. This sounds like a lot of work, but knitting a few extra rows is really no sweat if you go to the trouble of mending at all.

This old favorite sock is too good to throw away. The heel and gusset have been reknitted with a sturdy, Navajo-ply yarn spun from some leftover roving.

Locate the hole on the heel and mark the place where the surrounding yarn is still very sound. If this is inside the gusset area, remove the row two rows after the last decrease in the gusset, beginning at the center sole (see p. 61). Remove the foot section and lay it aside with either waste yarn or circular needles holding the loose sts.

Unravel the heel all the way to the top of the placket. With new sound yarn, knit the heel and gusset, then graft the top part of the sock onto the foot part with Kitchener stitch. This really is easier than it sounds. I like to leave the sts from the foot part on waste yarn and the sts from the upper part on four dp needles during grafting. Make sure that you begin and end at the center sole line.

**AFTERTHOUGHT HEELS** I hesitated to take up sock knitting because I go through heels pretty quickly. It bugged me to think of doing all that work just to have it wear out in one spot, but after I wore my first pair of handknit, handspun socks, I had to keep making more because they were so comfortable.

Although it is possible to prolong the life of a sock by mending it with duplicate stitch, I prefer to replace heels, not

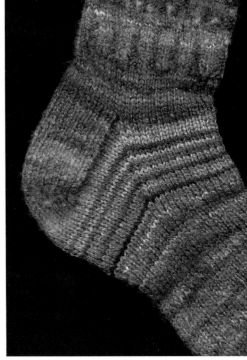

photo: Lynne Vogel

mend them. Afterthought heels, or heels that are added to a tube, are especially easy to take out and reknit, so I've put several variations on that theme, along with replacement directions, in this section.

Here's another good reason for making afterthought heels. Have you ever wanted to surprise someone with a pair of socks without knowing their size? Since the circumference of a person's foot is easy to accommodate with stretch and fairly easy to guess, it's possible to start knitting and get a good head start on a pair without knowing the person's foot length. Often in the time it takes to knit the pair, one can surreptitiously find out the proper length without the recipient being any the wiser. With the

▶ After marking the center stitch of the row to be removed, put the stitches from the rows on either side on two circular needles. Once the center row has been removed it is easy to notice that one row has an odd number of stitches and one has an even number of stitches.

afterthought heel, you can knit an entire pair before you have to commit to heel placement.

**Starting an afterthought heel** To insert an afterthought heel, you will open a hole in a tube that's already knit and pick up sts around the opening. You will need two circular needles (CN1 and CN2) the same size or smaller than the size used to knit the sock.

1. Mark the center back of the tube between the two center sts.

2. Measure the position of the heel and mark the row you want to remove at the center sole. If the sock is finished to the toe (except of course for the heel), try it on and measure the row that falls at the instep line or go by a measurement you've already taken (p. 55). Point the toe when measuring. Add about ¼" (6 mm) for "breathing room."

3. With CN1, begin at the center line of the row on the cuff side of the row to be removed and pick up one-fourth of the sts in the complete round, plus 2 sts. Slide the needle through the sts so that its other end is near the center back, then use it to pick up the same number of sts in the same row,

on the other side of the center line. Work straight across. Center all these sts on CN1. It is now your stitch holder.

4. With CN2, pick up sts from the row on the toe side of the marked row. The sts in this row will be offset from those in the row to be removed, and there will be one extra st in the center back. Insert CN2 into that center st, then pick up the same number of sts on each side as you did with CN1. (Note: If the sock was knitted from the toe up, the odd-numbered row will be on the cuff end rather than the toe end.)

photo: Lynne Vogel

## MENDING SOCK HEELS

With duplicate stitch, it is possible to mend a sock that hasn't worn all the way through, as long as you work well into the sound part surrounding the worn area. But if you only work the worn area, the juncture between the stitches you have worked and the ones you haven't will soon give out, tearing the duplicate stitch patch away from the rest of the sock. For this reason I prefer to reknit worn heels and toes. ◈

▶ When mending a worn heel with duplicate stitch, work new stitches well into the remaining sound fabric.

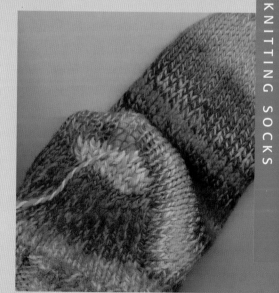

photo: Lynne Vogel

KNITTING SOCKS

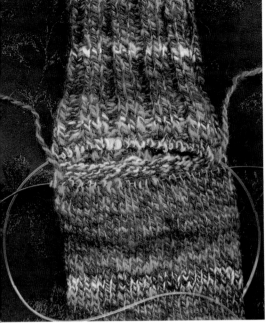

◀ The center row has been removed and the unraveled tails lie on each side. It is now time to transfer the stitches to four double-pointed needles.

Prepare to knit in the round by transferring the stitches from CN1 equally onto two dp needles. Do the same with the sts from CN2. (There will be one extra st on one of the four dp needles.)

Attach yarn and knit 1 rnd. K2tog on the needle that carries the extra st. Work decs as follows:

*Rnd 1:* On N1 and N3, knit to last 3 sts, k2tog, k1. On N2 and N4, k1, ssk, knit across.

*Rnds 2 and 3:* Knit around.

Repeat these three rnds until heel reaches desired depth. It is usually sufficient to knit until the opening is 1¼ inches (3.2 cm) across. For a shallow heel, dec every second rnd instead of every third rnd. Graft remaining sts with Kitchener st.

5. Clip the center st of the row to be removed. With a blunt needle or knitting needle, unravel the row st by st toward the corners of the heel on both sides. Leave the unraveled tail in the last st of each row, top and bottom. You will use the unraveled yarn later to close any gaps at the corners when finishing.

### Knitting the afterthought wedge heel
This is a very comfortable heel and gives a good fit on a shallow heel. It is very simple to knit. As Elizabeth Zimmermann says, you just knit a (wedge) toe.

▶ The afterthought wedge heel. Stephanie plied the multicolored wool roving with a solid black Merino for the body of the sock, and plied the roving onto itself for the toe and heel. She knit the future heel opening in white cotton.

▲ Afterthought center-decrease heel.

### Knitting the afterthought center-decrease heel
This heel mimics the hourglass heel but is easier to knit. The decreases may feel a bit bulky, but most people don't notice that when wearing the sock.

Begin as for wedge heel. Work decs as follows:

*Rnd 1:* On N1 and N3, knit. On N2 and N4, knit to the last 2 sts. Sl 2 kwise, sl the first st from the next needle kwise, return these 3 sts to the left needle, sl1, k2tog, psso.

*Rnd 2:* Knit around.

Repeat these two rnds until heel reaches desired depth. Graft remaining sts with Kitchener st.

**Knitting the afterthought hourglass heel** For those who prefer a true hourglass heel, here is an afterthought version. It makes the perfect replacement for the worn-out, knit-as-you-go version. This heel is knit back and forth and then grafted to the heel opening in the sock with Kitchener st. Since this heel is symmetrical, it can be knitted toe up or cuff down and is the same either way.

**Begin the heel shaping** One CN will have an odd number of sts. Count them and mark the center st. Use these sts to work your heel. Leave the sts on the other CN in reserve until the heel is knitted.

*Row 1 (RS):* With a dp needle, knit to the center point and k2tog (the cen-

ter st with the one before it), then knit across.

*Row 2 (WS):* Purl across.

*Row 3:* Knit to last st. Turn, leaving that st on the left needle.

*Row 4:* Yo pwise, purl across to the last st. Turn, leaving that st on the left needle.

Continue, as for regular hourglass heel (see p. 51). Your next st will be a YO. When all possible decs have been made, there should be the same number of sts on the needles as there were in the beginning of the heel. This number should match the number of reserved sts on the cable needle.

Measure and break off several feet of the working yarn. Thread a BN and graft remaining sts with Kitchener st.

Using the reserved ends from the removed row, thread them into a BN and close any holes at the corner of the heels with appropriate camouflage.

**Replacing afterthought heels** Heels often wear out while the rest of the sock looks almost new. The fastidious heel

mender must be ready to do some creative dismantling.

Afterthought heels are really easy to fix if the hole is on the actual heel part. If you are planning to reknit the entire heel, pick up the sts of the row before the first row of the heel. This is one reason to knit heels with a contrasting color, because it makes that row so easy to find.

◈ To mend afterthought center-decrease heels and afterthought wedge heels, put the picked-up sts on four dp needles just as they were before you knit the heel. Make sure the needles are positioned with N1 and N4 meeting at the center back. Then fold the heel in half and cut the tip off with sharp scissors. Unravel the heel up to the needles and knit a new one in its place.

◈ To mend afterthought hourglass heels, put the sts of the row where you first knitted the heel onto two dp needles, just as they were when you began to knit it in the first place. (Using two needles simply makes the sock more workable during the unraveling. When you are ready to knit the heel, you can return to one needle.) Find the first complete round after the

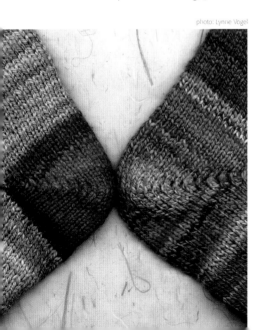

◀ Right: A knit-as-you-go hourglass heel. Left: An afterthought hourglass heel. Can you tell the difference?

heel, and with a BN, slip waste yarn through those sts. If you knitted the heel in a contrasting color, make sure to pick up the sts of the last row in the main color. To remove the old heel, clip the last row of the heel (the row nearest the row on waste yarn) and pull out that row one st at a time. Unravel the rest of the heel up to the needles and knit a new one in its place.

◈ Regular hourglass heels can be mended the same way as afterthought hourglass heels. When you unravel the first row, you will see a k3tog decrease on either side of the row you are unraveling. Just remove those sts and reknit with afterthought heel.

**BASIC SOCK TOES** Both wedge and round toes are easy to knit. I like the comfort of round toes and the tailored look of wedges. Try them both and see which you prefer.

The round toe is handy when knitting tube socks. Since it fits the foot in any direction, the sock with a round toe can be shifted to any position on the foot. This makes knitting with energized singles or spiral patterns easier, since the

▶ Stephanie's wedge toe (left) and Sandy's round toe (right).

toe doesn't have to line up with the heel. Another plus—you won't have to work Kitchener stitch! This is a great toe for beginning sock knitters.

Replacing toes is easy. Be sure to start in a spot where the knitting is still sound. Mark that row by putting the sts onto four dp needles (see p. 61). Cut off the toe below this round and unravel up to your needles. Knit the new toe of your choice.

**Wedge toe** This familiar toe shaping is serviceable, easy to work, and comfortable. Begin at center back 2" (5 cm) from desired finished length with working sts evenly divided on four dp needles.

*Rnd 1:* On N1 and N3, knit to last 3 sts, k2tog, k1. On N2 and N4, k1, ssk, knit across.

*Rnd 2:* Knit around.

Repeat these two rnds until 4 sts remain on each needle. Graft remaining sts with Kitchener st.

**Round toe** This toe shaping is only about 1½" (3.8 cm) long, so I add an extra ½" (1.3 cm) to the foot before beginning a round toe. Begin at center back with working sts evenly divided on four dp needles. Don't worry if there are

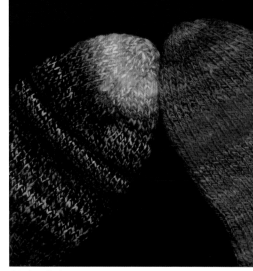

a few sts left over at the end of a dec rnd—the shaping turns out okay anyway.

*Dec rnd 1:* *K4, k2tog* around. Knit 4 rnds.

*Dec rnd 2:* *K3, k2tog* around. Knit 3 rnds.

*Dec rnd 3:* *K2, k2tog* around. Knit 2 rnds.

*Dec rnd 4:* *K1, k2tog* around. Knit 1 rnd.

*Dec rnd 5:* K2tog around. Break yarn and finish with simple bind off.

**FANCY TOES** Thong toes and piggy toes present a bit more challenge to the knitter both in knitting and fit. When knitting piggy toes, I look like I'm holding a porcupine. Nevertheless, they are fun to knit and even more fun to wear. They not only keep the feet warmer than ordinary socks but make slipping on sandals for a quick trip to the mailbox a lot more fun.

**Thong toe sock** This sock is like a mitten for the foot. It has a fourchette—a gusset that fits snugly between the big toe and the other four toes to accommodate the thong of a sandal. This pattern fits women's size medium if knitted with yarn that measures 11 or 12 wraps per inch with size 3 (3.25 mm) needles.

If knitting from the cuff down, work as usual until the foot is 2" (5 cm) shorter than desired finished length. These directions call for 56 working sts equally divided on four

 Lynne designed these socks to wear with her thongs.

photo: Lynne Vogel

Twisted Sister Laurie makes this toe on socks for her sister who has diabetes. This toe looks long and pointy until you put it on, when it becomes roomy and comfortable. Her sister claims that they are the only socks that allow her enough circulation to her toes. Simply work a wedge toe and keep decreasing until you have only 8 sts remaining. Finish with simple bind off.

Note the beautiful color effects in these socks. Twisted Sister Laurie spins very thin yarn. She often wants a heavier fabric than one that can be knit with one strand alone. She finds that combining two strands of the same yarn can give unexpected and beautiful results. Knitting yarns together like this is a good way to blend variegated yarns and expand your color palette. You can homogenize wild or uneven variegations or add a unifying element such as a strand of a solid color. ◈

▼ Laurie's Magic Genie-toe socks.

photo: Jim Ann Howard

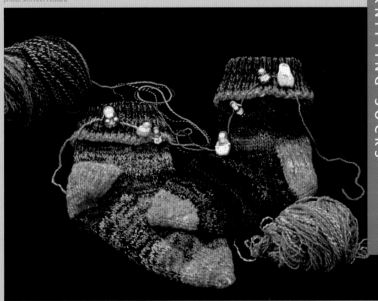

**KNITTING SOCKS**

photo: Lynne Vogel

The fourchette between the big and second toes for thong toe only.

needles. (As with the basic sock, I number these needles N1 to N4.) To knit a thong toe sock from the toe up, I begin with a provisional cast-on row of 56 sts, knit down the two toe sections, then pick up sts along the cast-on row and knit up the foot.

**Setup** The following directions are for a right sock. For the left sock, begin at center bottom instead of center top. Needles 3, 4, 1, and 2 become needles 1, 2, 3, and 4. Then follow directions for the right sock.

Starting at center back, knit all sts on N1 and N2. Knit 6 sts on N3, leaving 8 sts. Transfer those 8 sts and the first 8 sts from N4 onto waste yarn.

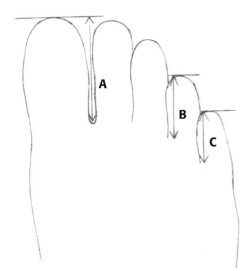

A

B

C

## Outer toe section

*Rnd 1:* Return to N3. CO 6 sts with a simple cast on. With new needle, knit across the sts on N4. Transfer 3 of the cast-on sts from N3 to N4. Now N3 and N4 each have 9 sts.

*Rnd 2 and all even rows:* Knit.

*Rnd 3:* On N1, knit across to last 3 sts, k2tog, k1. On N2, k1, ssk, knit across. On N3, k5, k2tog, k2. On N4, k2, ssk, k5.

*Rnd 5:* On N1, knit across to last 3 sts, k2tog, k1. On N2, k1, ssk, knit across.

On N3, k5, k2tog, k1. On N4, k1, ssk, k5.

*Rnd 7:* On N1, knit across to last 3 sts, k2tog, k1. On N2, k1, ssk, knit across. On N3, k5, k2tog. On N4, ssk, k5.

On remaining odd rounds, continue to dec on the outside of the foot (N1 and N2) until the outer toe section is 2" (5 cm) long or desired length. Join remaining sts with Kitchener st.

**Big toe section** I usually knit off three needles to work the big toe. Transfer 16 sts from waste yarn onto two needles,

◀ In your bare feet, stand on a sheet of paper and trace the outline of the toe half with a pencil, while putting full weight on your feet. It helps to have a friend draw while you stand.

**Line A.** Measure the lengths of the big and second toes from the bottom of the crook between them (pp. 83–84).

**Line B.** Measure the lengths of the third and fourth toes from the bottom of the crook between them (p. 84).

**Line C.** Measure the length of the little toe from the bottom of the crook between it and the fourth toe.
Measure the lengths of the toes on your socks from the same place as you measured them on your feet (p. 83).

Color PATTERNS in variegated

yarns can be unpredictable.

*Bending* the pattern to

accommodate the yarn

is often more successful than trying to

BEND the yarn to accommodate

the pattern.

—LYNNE'S TIP

putting 8 sts on each needle. With a third needle, pick up 7 sts along the cast-on edge of the fourchette. (If there are gaps between the cast-on sts and the foot sts, reach down and pick up an extra st on either side of the cast-on sts, choosing whichever loop best closes the gap. Picking up an extra st or two won't hurt. You can always k2tog if you find you have too many sts.) Needles are numbered as follows: N1 is the bottom of toe, N2 is the top side of toe, N3 is the fourchette. All rnds begin on N1.

*Rnd 1 and all odd rnds:* Knit around.

*Rnd 2:* On N1, knit. On N2, knit. On N3, k2tog, k5, ssk.

*Rnd 4:* On N1, knit. On N2, knit. On N3, k2tog, k3, ssk.

*Rnd 6:* On N1, knit. On N2, knit. On N3, k2tog, k1, ssk.

*Rnds 7–12:* Knit.

*Rnd 13:* K2tog at the center st of each needle.

*Rnds 14–16:* Knit.

*Rnd 17:* K2tog at the center of each needle.

Continue knitting until toe is 2" (5 cm) long or desired length. Divide remaining sts evenly between top and bottom and join with Kitchener stitch. Or if you prefer, k2tog around, knit 1 more rnd, and finish with a simple bind off by threading yarn tail through BN and weaving through each st, pull yarn gently to bring sts together and close top.

**Piggy toes** Piggy-toe socks are like gloves for the feet, without thumbs of course. Between the toes, the openings between the top and sole of the sock are spanned by small groups of cast-on stitches, called fourchettes.

It is nice to have at least two sets of four needles or a set of five and a circular needle for this pattern. Otherwise you will have to put stitches on waste yarn when you aren't working them.

These directions call for 60 working sts. The sock fits a women's size medium when worked on size 2 (2.75 mm) needles with yarn that measures about 13 wraps per inch (2.5 cm). This pattern is impractical for heavy yarn.

**Setup** The following directions are for a right sock. For the left sock, begin at center top instead of center bottom. Needles 3, 4, 1, and 2 become needles 1, 2, 3, and 4. Then follow directions for the right sock.

Knit foot of sock to 2½" (6.5 cm) from end of longest toe. Divide sts so that there are 14 sts each on N1 and N2 and 16 sts each on N3 and N4.

**Little toe** Beginning at center back, knit all sts on N1 and N2. Knit to the last 6 sts on N3. With a new needle, knit the last 6 sts on N3. With a new needle, knit

photo: Lynne Vogel

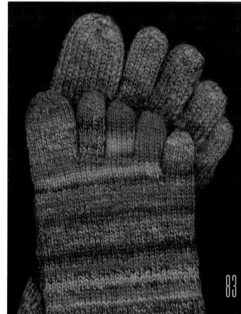

the first 6 sts of N4. With a new needle, CO 3 sts with loop cast on and join round to beginning of last 6 sts of N3. There will be 15 sts in the round, arranged on three needles.

Knit to the length of little toe. Dec by k2tog all around. Knit 1 more rnd and finish with simple bind off by threading yarn tail through BN and weaving through each st, pull yarn gently to bring sts together and close top.

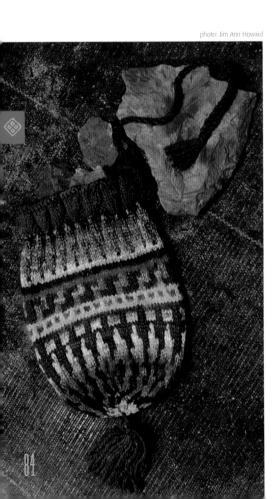

**Fourth toe** Beginning where you left off at N4, tie on yarn and knit all sts on N4, N1, N2, and N3. With N3, pick up 4 sts into the cast-on fourchette and join round. You should have 52 sts in all. Knit 4 rnds, ending at the beginning of N4.

Knit the first 5 sts of N4. With a new needle, CO 3 sts with loop cast on and join rnd as in little toe. Knit the last 9 sts of N3. You should have 17 sts. Redistribute the sts evenly on the needles.

Knit to length of fourth toe. Dec as before. Knit 1 more rnd and finish same as little toe.

**Third toe** Knit all the sts on N4, N1, N2, and N3. With N3, pick up 4 sts into the cast-on fourchette and join round.

Knit 2 rnds, ending at the beginning of N4.

Knit the last 5 sts on N4. With a new needle, CO 3 sts with loop cast on. Knit all the sts on N3. You should have 17 sts. Redistribute them evenly on the needles.

Knit to length of third toe. Dec as before. Knit 1 more rnd and finish same as previous toes.

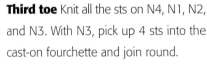

Debby's treasure bag.

**Second toe** Now all the sts are on N1 and N2. Knit the first 4 sts from N1*. With a BN, transfer the last 10 sts on N1 and the first 10 sts from N2 onto waste yarn. Return to * and with a new needle, CO 5 sts and join round to last 4 sts of N2. Pick up 4 sts into the cast-on loops of the fourchette and join round. You should have 17 sts. Divide them onto three needles.

Knit to length of second toe. Dec as before. Knit 1 more rnd and finish as previous toes.

**Big toe** Transfer sts from waste yarn onto N1 and N2. Knit those sts. With a

▶ Gail's baby socks.

new needle, pick up 6 sts into the fourchette. You will have 26 sts. Divide sts evenly on three needles (9-9-8).

Knit to two-thirds the length of the toe or to where it begins to narrow.

*Dec rnd:* K2tog once on each needle—23 sts rem..

Continue knitting to ¼" (6 mm) from end of toe. Dec by *k1, k2tog* around, end k2—16sts rem. Knit 4 more rows. K2tog around 8 sts rem. Finish same as previous toes.

**GALLERY** Welcome to the inspiration section. None of these socks was knit with a pattern. We all just figured it out as we went along.  Here's hoping you'll find color, ideas, and inspiration for designing your own.

**Treasure bags** Treasure bags are so much fun to knit. Use your most precious yarns or your tiny leftovers. A treasure bag is just a big cuff with a toe on it. What could be simpler? The best part is that you don't have to knit a mate!

**Baby socks** Gail knitted these baby-size socks from the cuff down on 40 sts. She chose a gusset heel and finished with a wedge toe, altering the decrease rounds

photo: Lynne Vogel

to make the toe short and wide. Gail says, "As I was knitting them I kept thinking about fall leaves, pine trees, and Japanese gardens (the red tones reminded me of the red lacquer bridges and the maples). The blues made me think of fall showers, and the earth tones make an awesome contrast to the brighter jewel tones. I had rainbows and leaves and sunsets and sunrises and a touch of Oregon rain all rolled up into these little baby socks!"

Gail wants to knit more and fill them with sachet, sew up the top of the cuff, and hang them in her closet. She has even toyed with the idea of stuffing one full of catnip for the cat.

**Unspun felted slippers** Jan knitted these slippers from unspun roving on size 10½ (6.5 mm) needles to make them larger than desired, then felted to return them to normal size and make them really durable. For more on this technique, see "Knitting with Unspun Roving," by Rita Buchanan, *Spin-Off* Fall 2000, pp. 50–53. These medium-size slippers weigh about 6 ounces (170 g).

Jan knitted from the cuff down on 40 working sts, knitting back and forth to form the opening, then joining the round and proceeding with a gusset heel and wedge toe. The simple slip stitch pattern is worked on a multiple of 4 sts. *Row 1:* K1, *k1, sl1 wyf*, k1.
*Rows 2 and 4:* Purl.
*Row 3:* K1, *sl1 wyf, k1*, k1.

To felt the slippers, put them in the washing machine on normal cycle in hot

photo: Lynne Vogel

◄ The felted slipper is much smaller and denser than the unfelted one. The roving is Corriedale wool. Jan sewed on a non-felted Navajo-ply seed stitch cuff after she felted the slipper.

water. After 5 minutes agitation, remove slippers and check their size. Continue briefly agitating and then checking until they have shrunk to the desired size. Then rinse the slippers well in hot water and lay them flat to dry.

**Socks with a stitch pattern** I knitted this sock in Old Shale stitch, using yarns from the Tide Pool series (p. 12). Old Shale is worked on a multiple of 11 sts so I used 6 repeats, or 66 sts. I started with an invisible cast on and knitted down. At the heel, I divided the sts in half and centered a repeat on the placket, then I picked up the gusset sts and worked them in stockinette stitch while maintaining the Old Shale pattern on the instep and sole of the sock. At the toe, I left one repeat at center top and one at center bottom and worked the toe decs in stockinette. Finally I returned to the cast-on row, picked up the sts, and worked two rows of garter st, finishing with a single crochet bind off.

▶ To give the Old Shale sock a three-dimensional look, Lynne changed yarn every four rows, repeating the same yarn every third time.

photo: Lynne Vogel

Here's the stitch pattern for Old Shale.

*Rnd 1:* Knit.

*Rnd 2:* Purl.

*Rnd 3:* K2tog twice; *M1, k1* three times, M1; k2tog twice.

*Rnd 4:* Knit.

### The antique sock knitting machine

Twisted Sister Gina is an expert collector of antique circular sock knitting machines. These machines have been made since 1869. Machines in Gina's collection date from the early 1900s to 1982. She has demonstrated the machine at the Black Sheep Gathering for the past several years.

photo: Lynne Vogel

photo: Lynne Vogel

Sock machines have a circular row of needles. As you turn a crank, the needles rise and fall on a cylinder and knit a tube. You make hourglass heels on them by lifting some of the needles out of action and knitting back and forth in short rows. A ribbing attachment fits atop the cylinder to make ribbing, so you can produce a factory-looking sock in a very short time.

Although these machines can be

◀ Gina is turning the crank on one of her sock knitting machines.

finicky, they are gaining in popularity and there are many enthusiasts and collectors. These machines were made by the thousands during World War I to mass-produce socks for the troops overseas. Many were lost to the metal drives of World War II, but thousands linger in attics, just waiting to be rediscovered by modern-day sock knitters!

Some machines were outfitted to make argyle patterns, polka dots, and lace. Gina is usually happy to get a pair of socks that match, no fancy add-ons required.

**WASHING HANDKNIT SOCKS** After putting so much care and time into making a pair of socks, it is wise to take as much care in laundering them. Some fibers and yarns are tougher than others and can go in the washing machine, but it's always wise to wash a pair by hand the first time or make a swatch and experiment with that. Socks made from densely spun and tightly knitted wool of any kind can be washed in the washing machine in COLD water on the gentle cycle, but lace socks should never go near a machine. Superwash wool can be machine-washed in either cold or warm water with your regular detergent. Generally you should avoid machine drying. A stocking bag is a good thing to use, especially when several people in a household help with laundry. The bag keeps the socks from overfuzzing and alerts anyone to set them aside and not just move them from the washer into the dryer.

Water temperature is a very important factor. To avoid shrinkage, use the same temperature of water throughout the washing process. This means you can use warm water to hand wash socks, as long as you rinse them in the same warm temperature. Use just enough soap or detergent to loosen dirt but not so much that the suds are difficult to rinse out. For hand washing, follow these steps:

❖ 1. Wash. Dissolve a small amount of soap such as a quick squirt of dish-washing detergent or shampoo in a small basin of warm water. Press the socks gently into the warm soapy water. Let soak 5 to 10 minutes. Squeeze gently to remove dirt. Squeeze all soapy water out of socks and lay aside.

❖ 2. Rinse. Remove dirty water from basin and refill with clean water at the same temperature. Press socks back into clean water. Let soak 1 minute, then squeeze gently until no more soap or dirt come out with the squeezing. Refill with clean water as many times as necessary. One rinse should do it if you used the right amount of soap and the socks weren't actually grungy.

❖ 3. Spin. Squeeze excess water out of socks by rolling them in a clean, dry bath towel and pressing down on them several times, or spin them in the washing machine on the spin cycle only. (Monitor or set the machine to avoid spraying water on the socks.) Spinning is essential in damp climates as it speeds drying time, sometimes by a full day.

❖ 4. Dry. Tug or pat the damp socks into shape. Lay socks flat to dry on a screen or dry towel, or hang over a towel rack or drying rack. Turn them inside out halfway through the drying process to speed drying of thick socks.

photo: Lynne Vogel

▶ Cindy spun a solid roving to set off the more subtle tones of the variegated yarn in this lovely Fair Isle sock. She made the pattern up as she went along and finished with Nancy Bush's star toe.

# SUPPLIERS

To save space, this list only includes companies we have actually traded with. There are many other wonderful sources out there. Check the weblists at the bottom for more sources near you.

## DYES AND RELATED EQUIPMENT

**Dharma Trading**
Box 150916
San Rafael, CA 94915
(800) 542-5227
www.dharmatrading.com
(Dyes and dyeing equipment)

**Earth Guild**
33 Haywood St.
Asheville, NC 28801
(800) 327-8448
www.earthguild.com
(Dyes, equipment, fibers)

**Cheryl Kolander, Aurora Silk**
5806 N. Vancouver Ave.
Portland, OR 97217
(503) 286-4149
www.Aurorasilk.com
(Natural dyes)

**Lab Safety Supply**
PO Box 1368
Janesville, WI 53547-1368
(800) 356-0783
www.labsafety.com
(All kinds of scientific supplies, containers, measuring devices and the catalog has a black LABrador) dog in a lab coat on the cover.)

**ProChem**
PO Box 14
Somerset, MA 02726
(888) 2-BUY-DYE   [(888) 228-9393]
www.prochemical.com
(Dyes and equipment)

**Julie Owens, Sheep Hollow Farm and Fiber**
24551 S. Metzler Park Rd.
Estacada, OR 97023
(503) 630-2317
www.sheephollow.iwarp.com
(Lanaset® dyes, "Lanaset Rainbows" dye sample book)

## FIBERS AND HANDPAINTED ROVINGS

**The Best of Wool**
7195 Palm Ave.
Sebastopol, CA 95472
(707) 824 9988
(Hand-dyed rovings and space-dyed yarn in beautiful colors)

**Pat Bullen, Bullen's Wullens**
5711 County Road #13
Centerburg, OH  43011
(800) 565 7290
www.BullensWullens.com
(CD Drop Spindle kit, wide array of solid color fibers)

**Chasing Rainbows Dyeworks**
1700 Hilltop Dr.
Willits, CA 95490
(707) 459 8558
(Hand-dyed rovings)

**Rosemary Wilkinson**
Dunnose Head Farm
Falkland Islands
South Atlantic
www.falklandwool.com
www.craftynotions.com
(Wool fiber and yarn for dyeing)

**Fantasy Fibers**
26516 S. Hwy. 170
Canby, OR 97013
(503) 263-4902
www.fantasyfibers.com
(Fiber, fiber processing)

**Stefania Isaacson, Fiber Artist**
41W395 Woodland Dr.
Saint Charles, Illinois 60175
(630) 377-5704
www.handspinning.com/stef
(Natural-dyed fiber)

**Lambspun of Colorado**
1101 E. Lincoln Ave.
Fort Collins, CO 80524
(800) 558-5262
lambspun@webaccess.net
(Undyed rovings)

**La Lana Wools**
136 Paseo Norte
Taos, NM 87571
(505) 758-9631
(888) 377-9631 orders only
www.lalanawools.com
(Natural-dyed fiber)

**Northwest Wools**
3524 S.W. Troy
Portland, OR 97219
(503) 244-5024
nwwools@ccwebster.net
(Cushing dyes, yarn for dyeing, books, hand-dyed fibers)

**Royal Hare**
946 Lodi St.
Santa Rosa, CA 95401
(707) 579-2344
www.royalehare.com
(Space dyed rovings in gorgeous colors)

**Twisted Sisters**
654 E. Sheridan Ave.
Escondido, CA 92029
(858) 350-9951
(Hand-dyed and handpainted yarns—not
to be confused with the Twisted Sisters
in this book.)

**Woolgatherings**
PO Box 132
Banks, OR 97106
www.woolgatherings.com
(Hand-dyed rovings, "Happy Socks" kit
for spinners and knitters)

**SPINDLES**
**Greensleeves Spindles**
4505 Canyon Rd.
Provo, UT 84604
(801) 226-7582
www.greensleevesspindles.com
(Handspindles)

**Jim Childs, Hatchtown Farm**
82 Sproul Hill Rd.
Bristol, ME 04539
(207) 563-5952
www.Hatchtown.com
(Handspindles)

**Jim Mitchell, Poppa's Art and Toys**
PO Box 143616
Austin, TX 78714-3616
(512) 928-8829
www.toys-n-art.com
(Handspindles)

**Tracy and Jean Eichheim, Woolly
Designs**
41285 Weld County Rd. 15
Ft. Collins, CO 80524-9106
(970) 484 0445
www.woollydesigns.com
(Handspindles)

**WEBLINKS**
**www.handspinning.com**

**www.socknitters.com**

**www.textilelinks.com**

**www.urbanspinner.com**

**www.thepiper.com/fiberart/koolaid
/images/colorchart-max.jpg**

# FURTHER READING

Bordi, Cat. *Socks Soar on Two Circular Needles.* Friday Harbor, Washington: Passing Paws Press, 2001.

Bush, Nancy. *Folk Socks: The History & Techniques of Handknitted Footwear, with 18 Exceptional Patterns.* Loveland, Colorado: Interweave Press, 1994.

Bush, Nancy. *Knitting on the Road: Sock Patterns for the Traveling Knitter.* Loveland, Colorado: Interweave Press, 2001.

Gibson-Roberts, Priscilla A. *Ethnic Socks & Stockings: A Compendium of Eastern Design & Technique.* Sioux Falls, South Dakota: XRX, 1997.

*A Handspindle Treasury: 20 years of Spinning Wisdom from Spin•Off Magazine.* Loveland, Colorado: Interweave Press, 2000.

Menz, Deb. *Color in Spinning.* Loveland Colorado: Interweave Press, 1998.

Rowley, Elaine. *Socks, Socks, Socks: 70 Winning Patterns From Knitter's Year of the Sock Contest.* Sioux Falls, South Dakota: XRX, 1998.

Zilboorg, Anna. *Simply Socks: 45 Traditional Turkish Patterns to Knit.* Asheville, North Carolina: Lark Books, 2001.

# INDEX